Thank you for purchasing this book. By doing so,
you are directly contributing to our work supporting
young people in Palestine through skateboarding.
We hope that you enjoy preparing these recipes as
much as we enjoyed collecting them.

This book is dedicated to Sajed Abu-Ulba.

شكرًا لقيامكم بشراء هذا الكتاب ، من خلال شرائكم هذا الكتاب قمتم
بالمساهمة في تعزيز قدرتنا على العطاء للشباب الفلسطيني ، نتمنى ان
تستمتعوا في تحضير الوصفات ، لأننا متأكدون أنها ستنال إعجابكم.

عائلة سكايت بال تهدي هذا الكتاب الى حياة ساجد ابو علبه.

"We
welco

The word 'shabab' is to mean 'youth' or 'youthfulness' but is most commonly used in reference to groups of teenage boys. Of all the greetings received in Palestine, the most energetic will undoubtedly come courtesy of the shabab. PHOTO BY TOM BIRD.

"Welcome to Palestine!" is a phrase guaranteed to greet you upon arrival in any Palestinian village, town or city. Then it's the famous hospitality, delicious food and beautiful scenery that makes visitors come back to this unique place time and time again.

Nestled between the eastern shore of the Mediterranean Sea and the Jordan River, Palestine has the perfect climate for growing an array of tasty produce, as well as year-round sunny skies - ideal for skateboarding!

Starting in 2013, SkatePal has run programmes throughout Palestine, using skateboarding as a tool to support the development of young people.

Since socio-political tensions and restrictions on freedom of movement mean that recreational opportunities in the country are severely limited, we run volunteer-led skateboarding classes across the West Bank. To date, we have built skateparks in a number of locations including Zebabdeh (2014), Asira Al-Shamaliya (2015) and Jayyous (2017), with plans to build a permanent community skateboard space in the cultural capital, Ramallah.

With the help of local and international volunteers, we are working towards creating a self-sustaining skateboarding scene that does not rely on international support.

lcome,
"
me.

Lujane, a relative of skatepark locals Sedra & Malak, enjoys mujadara (lentils & rice) in her family garden. 2019. PHOTO BY OWEN GODBERT.

So, what's food got to do with it?

Upon arriving in Palestine, it quickly becomes clear that food is sacred. Large shared plates bring people together to revel in stories and catch up on family news, whilst enjoying the delights of local produce. Over the past few years, this communal way of living has also come to encapsulate the vibe of the burgeoning local skateboarding scene.

Head down to the skatepark in the village of Asira Al-Shamaliya on a Friday afternoon and you will find the place packed not only with skateboarders of all ages, but families chilling among the hilltops drinking 'shay' (tea) or 'qahwa' (coffee), nibbling on sunflower seeds and smoking 'nargeela' (shisha).

Being a physically demanding sport, skate-boarders are known for big appetites to keep their energy levels up, and if you've got a big appetite, then Palestine is the place to be. The culture of food and coffee punctuate every meeting, family occasion and street mission: from a pre-session falafel wrap at Ramallah Plaza, to a mid-session plate of kanafeh when craving a sugar-hit, and finally to a post-session hearty home cooked meal with the entire family.

'Sahten' – which translates literally to 'two healths' – is commonly used when tucking into a meal. The traditional response 'A'la qalbak'

('on your heart') shows just how intertwined food and community are in Palestine.

The recipes in this book have been collected from various figures close to Palestine's growing skateboard community. These are supplemented with a couple of recipes from past volunteers and even by Palestine's own international master chef, Sami Tamimi. Some dishes are easy to make, serving as a quick bite before you hit the streets (SHAKSHUKA, P.40), some are heavier meals that take longer to prepare and are better enjoyed after the session (MAQLUBAH, P.140), and some are perfect anytime of day (FALAFEL, P.60). There's also something for those with a sweet tooth (KANAFEH, P.148) and for the coffee addicts too (QAHWA ARABIA, P.34).

Sandwiched between the recipes are interviews with local and professional skaters, as well as various features that help build a bit more of a picture of Palestine. There is even a yoga sequence designed to help ease any skate-re-lated aches and pains. You don't have to ride a skateboard in order to appreciate these recipes, but for the full SkatePal experience, we'd suggest you give it a try.

Finally, a quick note on dietary requirements... Whilst most dishes are vegetarian, many signature Palestinian dishes include meat.

This book aims to bring an authentic piece of Palestine to your table, directly from the community that we work with, so we've therefore kept the recipes in their true form. However, a little online research will reveal tips that can make classic dishes vegetarian-friendly.

A huge thanks to everyone who has contributed to this book (full list of credits at the back) and to our work in Palestine over the past few years. We would also like to thank you, dear reader; by purchasing this book you are directly helping to ensure that the Palestinian skate scene is sustainable for future generations.

We hope you enjoy the stories and recipes in this book as much as we've enjoyed collecting them, and we'd encourage you to visit Palestine – whether that be as a tourist, a skater (get in touch for tips & contacts), or even as part of our volunteer programme.

OK, introductions over, time to get some water boiling and turn to page 34 to brew yourself some traditional Qahwa Arabia!

Sahten!

SkatePal

Mohammed's constant supply of fresh tea with mint
contains a spoonful of sugar large enough to keep
the sessions at Asira Al-Shamaliya skatepark going
well into the evening. PHOTO BY TOM BIRD

Contents:

When it's time to skate, the minds and spirits of the Asira Al-Shamaliya locals run wild against the backdrop of rolling hills and neighbouring villages. **2019.** PHOTO BY WILL JIVCOFF.

Imagine your store cupboard as the nuts and bolts of a skateboard: they may appear small and insignificant, but they're what hold everything together. We'd recommend sourcing these ingredients from a local independent international or Arabic supermarket – you'll be more likely to find everything, and the price will be lower than the big chains. Alternatively, for a list of stockists offering fair trade Palestinian products, please refer to the back pages of this book. The following list is quite basic, but it'll cover you for the recipes in this book, and stand you in good stead to tackle many other popular Middle Eastern dishes.

A ALLSPICE
Made from the ground dried berries of the pimenta plant, allspice is indispensable in the Middle East and is used to season stews and meats.

ALMONDS
A popular nut used in both savoury and sweet dishes. Often bought whole and 'blanched' to remove the skin. See Fattet Makdous, for example.

B BAY LEAVES
Bay leaves are often used in cooking for their distinctive flavour and fragrance. They can be bought fresh or dried, but fresh have a much stronger flavour.

BULGUR WHEAT
Cracked whole wheat that has been par-boiled, dried and ground so it's easy and quick to cook. You'll probably be familiar with it in classic tabbouleh dishes.

C CARDAMOM
Cardamom can be bought in pods or ground. Typically only the seeds are used (unless stated otherwise). Cardamom has a spicy and sweet flavour unlike any other spice.

CAYENNE PEPPER
Long, thin and bright red. Usually purchased ground and used to add a fiery kick and piquant flavour. Use with caution!

CHICKPEAS
A staple ingredient in the Levantine diet used to make classics such as falafel and hummus and added to stews, salads, pilafs etc. Dried and canned varieties can be found in most supermarkets. Dried chickpeas are best, but dont forget they need to be soaked overnight in double their mass of water.

CINNAMON
An aromatic, heady and sweet spice, popular in sweet pastries, desserts and drinks. Also brilliant for adding extra depth to savoury stews.

CHILLI FLAKES
Dried crushed or ground chilli peppers, used to add flavour and heat to dishes. Various types are available for different heats and flavours.

CUMIN
Available to buy as whole seeds or ground, cumin has a strong, distinctive aroma and flavour and is the don daddy of spices.

D DATES
Dates are synonymous with Palestine. Grown on the date palm tree, much like a bunch of grapes, they can be eaten at various stages of ripeness. And while they're typically stocked partially dehydrated, you don't have to stand on a street corner in Palestine to get them fresh. If you can find them, the sweet, sticky, caramel flavour is well worth the search.

F FAVA BEANS (a.k.a. broad beans)
A staple in Middle Eastern cooking. They've been cultivated since ancient times and are still going strong! Best harvested when young and sweet, you can buy these fresh or dried. Fava beans are used in soups, purees, salads and stews like the iconic breakfast dish of champions: ful medames.

FETA
Rich and creamy, feta cheese is a soft and brined curd traditionally made with sheep or goat's milk, but there are some great vegan alternatives out there too.

FREEKEH
Popular in Middle Eastern cooking, freekeh is a young green wheat that's roasted and cracked. It has a smokey, nutty flavour and a good bite to it.

L LABNEH
Labneh is made by straining yoghurt through muslin cloth. What you're left with is super thick, yoghurt cheese which is often rolled into balls. A regular accompaniment to pretty much all Palestinian dishes.

N NUTMEG
A gentle and earthy spice which goes really well with greens. It's best to buy it whole and grate it yourself as it has a much more vibrant flavour. Go easy though, it can be overpowering if you use too much.

O OLIVE OIL
Not all olive oil is created equal. There are many kinds of varying greatness. Arguably some of the best comes freshly pressed following the Palestinian olive harvest (more on that later). Our recommended supplier would be Zaytoun – a social enterprise which sells fairtrade Palestinian products (www.zaytoun.org). The fruity, peppery flavour is an essential part of Palestinian cooking, but remember, the purer the oil the lower the smoking point, so you're best opting for regular olive oil – rather than extra virgin – when frying with it.

OREGANO
Oregano is a herb plant, the leaves of which can be bought fresh or dried – both are great. It has a similar flavour to its cousin, marjoram, which you'll often find added to savoury vegetable and meat dishes.

P PINE NUTS
These are the kernels extracted from pine trees. They're small but pack a big flavour. For more warmth and nuttiness, toast them lightly.

PISTACHIOS
Pistachios are native to the Middle East and are part of the 'cashew' family. They're super high in protein (one of the most nutritious nuts), can be eaten on their own, lightly salted, or crushed and sprinkled over desserts such as kanafeh.

POMEGRANATE MOLASSES
A pleasantly intense thick syrup made from condensed pomegranate juice. Pomegranate molasses adds acidity and sweetness to salads, stews and soups.

S SEMOLINA
Semolina is ground durum wheat kernels. It's most commonly used in making fresh pasta, though you'll find it a key ingredient in some Levantine desserts, such as kanafeh (featured later in this book).

SUMAC
Dark, burgundy coloured berries are ground into a powder which add a sour and citrus punch to dishes. They are one of the ingredients in Palestine's famous spice mix za'atar (listed in this glossary). As with all spices, even when dried, you want them as fresh as possible. Sumac should be super vibrant in colour and almost moist to the touch, rather than dry and powdery.

T TAHINI
A Middle Eastern staple, tahini is made from toasted, ground, hulled sesame seeds. Both hummus and halva cannot exist without it.

TURMERIC
Warm and earthy with bitter undertones, this eye-popping yellow spice is used to add flavour and colour. It has enjoyed a resurgence in recent years across cafes and juice bars due to its 'superfood' properties.

V VERMICELLI
Vermicelli is a type of pasta, similar to spaghetti but much thinner. In Middle Eastern cooking, these often short (2-3 cm in length) 'noodles' are added to rice dishes and pilafs for a toasted flavour and sometimes used also in desserts e.g. in some versions of Nablus' legendary kanafeh.

Z ZA'ATAR
Za'atar is a variety of wild thyme that grows in abundance across Palestine, though its name most commonly refers to Palestine's most famous spice blend consisting of thyme, sumac and sesame seeds. Used to season vegetable and meat dishes, sprinkled over eggs, or dunked with oil-soaked taboon bread. When it comes to za'atar, almost anything goes.

[LEFT] **A butcher, Bethlehem.** [RIGHT] **A baker, Nablus.** PHOTOS BY TOM BIRD.

Behind every oven spilling freshly baked taboon breads out into the streets and hands of eager customers is a team of skillful makers. Ayub is one of them. Ramallah, 2019. PHOTO BY TOM BIRD.

'TABOON'

The most traditional flatbread in Palestine, named after the 'taboon' oven which was historically constructed out in the fields using mud and animal dung. First moulded into a dome shape similar to a pizza oven, stones would then be gathered and placed at the base where a fire was built. Once the fire had died down, dough would be laid over the scorching hot stones. This is what would give taboon bread the signature 'bumps' that distinguish it from other types of bread. Rugged and chewy, taboon bread will be found accompanying dishes such as shakshuka and mussakhan, and in the West Bank you'll commonly find it proudly displayed in front of bakeries, topped with za'taar and olive oil.

'MARKOOK'

This is the name most familiar across Palestine, though names such as 'khubz', 'saj' or even 'lavash' abound depending on the region within the Levant. Whatever the name, the thin, translucent, crepe-like bread is a Middle Eastern staple. After being stretched across the hot steel 'saj' for just a couple of seconds on either side, wide stacks of 10-20 pieces are folded into plastic bags. You'll find markook bread in our mansaf recipe, but its tearable quality makes it a perfect substitute for cutlery when eating ful medames, mezze or any other finger food.

'PITTA'

As the most globally recognised Arabic flatbread, the humble pitta probably requires little introduction. Its prevalence is no doubt a result of its versatility. Either ripped and dipped into tapenades, used to hold anything from falafel to souvlaki, or shredded and toated for the base of fattat makdous – the Palestinian breakfast is not complete without a towering pile of fresh pitta.

Following a chance meeting with some SkatePal volunteers in 2016, Ibtesam & her brother
Ahmed are often known to open their garden to anyone with a skateboard and a curiosity for
her sesame seed bread. Asira Al-Shamaliya, 2019. PHOTO BY OWEN GODBERT.

For many people, Palestine might not appear like a natural holiday destination.

This is largely due to how mainstream media outlets tend to report on the country and the wider Middle East. Yet spread across the country are the holiest sites of the three main monotheistic religions – Islam, Judaism and Christianity – and as such, thousands make the pilgrimage to this region each year.

For Christians, top of the itinerary is the biblical birthplace of Jesus – Bethlehem – situated a short journey south of Jerusalem in the Palestinian West Bank. It is a place which has been systematically crippled over a number of years – politically, geographically and economically – due, in part, to US foreign policy.

With that in mind, it almost seems to add insult to injury to ascend from Bethlehem's main bus terminal and be met with an image spring-loaded with all the symbolism of corporate America – the Starbucks logo. However, on second glance, not everything is quite as it seems. Rather than being seduced by a familiar caffeinated mermaid, customers are instead met with a slightly different logo: not Starbucks, but Stars & Bucks.

Most tourists pick up a coffee (or opt for a freshly pressed pomegranate juice – a refreshment more characteristic of the region) and eagerly browse the novelty Stars & Bucks porcelain mugs, snapping an obligatory selfie and indulging in a piece of familiarity out here on the fringes of the desert.

Stars & Bucks is Palestinian owned and operated, and in addition to the Bethlehem outlet, has two other cafes in the West Bank: Ramallah and Nablus. It is rare, however, that these cities play host to the throngs of tourists who pass through the Palestinian territory, whose eyes are set only on the holy sites of Bethlehem, Nazareth or Jericho.

It is equally unlikely therefore, that these same swathes of people will book their excursions through Palestinian tour operators, making it difficult to assess how much of the revenue generated through tourism actually filters back into Bethlehem and the surrounding West Bank.

With that in mind, Stars & Bucks is a sweet, if small, Palestinian victory within a larger narrative that rarely plays in their favour.

STARS & BUCKS CAFE

No religious pilgrimage is complete without a latte macchiato, right? PHOTO BY TOM BIRD

Qahwa Arabia

– by AL AMAD & SONS COFFEE (NABLUS)
العمد و اولاده

One of the key distinctions of Arabic coffee (and which makes it smell extra banging!) is that the beans are ground with cardamom. According to Izzeldin Bukhari – founder of Sacred Cuisine, and featured later in this book – cardamom has a long history as a symbol of status and honour in the Arab world. A traditional Bedouin folk song – later popularised by the famous Lebanese singer Samira Tawfiq – sings:

> *please pour the coffee*
> *and add to it more cardamom*
> *give it to the brave men*
> *on the back of horses.*

So if you've always dreamt of becoming a brave horseman, then look no further...

Al Amad & Sons العمد و اولاده is a family-run coffee roastery in Nablus' Old Town. For the past 40 years, various members of the family have operated the grinder, turning out the enticing scent of freshly roasted beans into the streets of Nablus. Competing against wafts of kanafeh and shawarma, the scent continues to lure locals and visiting skaters alike to the Al Amad storefront.

[LEFT] **Muhaned from Al Amad & Sons sits in front of the shop's roaster. Very few pieces of machinery smell this good.**

[RIGHT] **The Al Amad & Sons shopfront. Nablus Old City, 2019.** PHOTOS BY TOM BIRD.

– 250g **WHOLE COFFEE BEANS**
– 10–25g **CARDAMOM PODS**

SERVES: **2-3**
PREP TIME: **10 MINS**

For readers in Europe or America, you'll be most familiar with preparing coffee at home using either a French press cafetiere, a percolator, or a paper filter, which separates the coffee from the grounds. Arabic coffee, however, is served with the grounds. This means that your fate – whether you end up with a mouthful of coffee grounds or not – rests on your final sip. Believe us though, the heightened stakes are worth the risk.

1.   If using your own coffee grinder, grind the coffee beans and cardamom together. If you don't have a coffee grinder, simply head over to your local coffee spot, select the coffee beans you like (Al Amed and Sons source theirs from Tanzania) and ask your barista to grind them with your whole cardamom pods.

Al Amad & Son's recommend mixing between 10–25g of cardamom seeds into a standard 250g bag of coffee. So a ratio of 1:10 is a good rule of thumb.

2.   Qahwa Arabia is traditionally prepared in a 'dallah' (a stainless steel jug with a long handle - see illustration). You can usually find these in your local Arabic supermarket, but if that's a stretch, a small saucepan works just as well.

3.   For a medium pot (approx 2-3 cups), add 3 heaped tablespoons of the ground coffee and cardamom to cold water and stir.

4.   Hold over a high flame and bring to the boil. Once it begins to bubble up, remove the pot from the heat just before it spills over the edge. Then return it to the heat and find a position where it maintains a rolling boil for a few extra seconds.

5.   Leave to stand for a couple of minutes (allow the grounds to sink to the bottom) then pour slowly to avoid ending up with too many grounds in the cup.

[LEFT] Qahwa is often enjoyed with sunflower seeds. Lots of them. PHOTO BY TOM BIRD.
[RIGHT] A Jayyousi kid enjoys a cup of the strong stuff. 2018. PHOTO BY REID ALLEN.

Shakshuka

Abu Ali's shakshuka has become somewhat of a tradition among the SkatePal community. Multiple groups of volunteers have joined him for an early morning hike up to the 'Beit Zeki' tree – which roughly translates to 'home of the sweet things'. From the village it can be seen proudly crowning the top of the hill, sloping to one side in its uniquely relaxed way. Abu Ali runs a slick operation, somehow muscling a group of skaters to the top in time for the sun to creep over the horizon, conveniently providing enough light for everyone to begin gathering firewood. By the time everyone has found a rock that best fits the shape of their butt, Abu Ali's fire has already brought a pot of water to the boil. Dried sage and spoonfuls of sugar soon follow, as everyone gazes across rolling beige hills, inhaling the unmistakable scent of fresh tomatoes as they hit the pan with a loud crackle.

– by ABU ALI SAWALMA

ابو علي سوالمة

(ASIRA AL-SHAMALIYA)

Abu Ali Sawalma ابو علي سوالمة is one of the original skaters in Asira Al-Shamaliya. He put down his beloved mountain bike in 2015 – when the skatepark was just complete – to step on a skateboard for the first time, and has been a regular face there ever since. If you're lucky enough for his Uncle Suleiman to pass by when you're en route to the skatepark, he'll be the first to encourage you to cling to the back of his tractor while he tows you to the top.

– **5-6 EGGS**
– **8-10 RIPE TOMATOES**
  (ROUGHLY CHOPPED)
– **1 CAYENNE OR JALEPEÑO CHILLI**
  (THINLY SLICED)
– **2 TBSP ZA'TAAR**
– **GOOD QUALITY OLIVE OIL**
– **FEW SPRIGS OF PARSLEY**
  (ROUGHLY CHOPPED)
– **5-6 TABOON BREADS**
  (OR SIMILAR ARABIC FLATBREAD)
– **SALT & PEPPER**

SERVES: **4-5**
PREP TIME: **30 MINS**

1. Add a healthy glug of oil to a large frying pan and set it on a medium flame (Abu Ali's is made over an open fire, but you should generally avoid cooking olive oil at too high a temperature). When it begins to spit, chuck in the tomatoes – they should sizzle as they hit the pan. Give them a quick stir, then set to a low flame and leave to reduce.

2. After approx 10 minutes the tomatoes should have softened to a thick paste. Add the chilli and seeds to the pan (it'll give the shakshuka a good kick, whilst not being overpowering). Create some wells in the mixture and fill them one-by-one by cracking the eggs in. Abu Ali is more of a stir-it-all-in kinda guy, but if you'd prefer to leave the eggs whole, that's fine too.

3. Remove the pan from the heat whilst the eggs are still slightly undercooked. Cover the pan with a lid – the heat will finish cooking the eggs, while you heat the taboon bread in the oven and pick some parsley leaves. Alternatively you can turn a couple of pitta breads over the flame on the stove until they inflate.

4. Finish by scattering some parsley leaves over the pan, then rip some pieces of bread and dive straight into the shakshuka. Cutlery is not necessary here – this is food made for the fields!

Abu Ali Sawalma preparing his crack-of-dawn shakshuka under the 'Beit Zeki' tree. PHOTOS BY TOM BIRD.

SHAKSHUKA

Abu Ali climbing 'Beit Zeki' – the area's prime picnic spot, so long as you've got the legs to make it up the hill. 2017. PHOTO BY TOM BIRD.

- **800G FAVA/BROAD BEANS** (2 TINS)
- **1 RED CHILLI** (THINLY SLICED)
- **5 GARLIC CLOVES** (CRUSHED)
- **1 ONION** (DICED)
- **2 RIPE TOMATOES** (DICED)
- **1 LEMON** (JUICED)
- **1 TSP CUMIN**
- **SALT & PEPPER**
- **GOOD GLUG OF OLIVE OIL**
- **½ BUNCH OF PARSLEY**
  (FINELY CHOPPED)
- **TABOON BREAD**
  (OR SIMILAR ARABIC FLATBREAD)

SERVES: **3-4**
PREP TIME: **30 MINS**

1.   *The authentic way:* Source some dried fava beans and soak them in water overnight (same as you would for chickpeas when making falafel or hummus). The following day, simply replace the water, boil until the skin begins to peel away, drain, then remove the skins.

The lazy way: Empty the tinned fava beans (with liquid) into a pot, top up with water and bring to the boil.

2.   Drain the beans and set aside. Add a good splash of olive oil to the empty pot and return it to the heat. Add the onion, fry for 3 minutes, then add the garlic and chilli and cook for a further minute before adding the drained beans back in. Stir to coat everything.

3.   Add the tomatoes along with the cumin and a pinch of salt and pepper. Stir and allow to stew for approx 10 minutes.

4.   Cook until you're able to mash the mixture with the back of a spoon. Then add half of the chopped parsley and add a dash of water if the mix is drying out.

5.   Once the mixture has a good consistency (neither runny or clumpy) tip into a serving bowl, pour over the lemon juice, drizzle over a good amount of olive oil and scatter the remainder of the parsley. Warm the taboon bread, then use it to scoop up that delicious mush.

Ful Medames

– by TESSA FOX

Tessa Fox is a skater from Australia, who has spent recent years living between the Palestinian Occupied Territories and Turkey working as a freelance journalist for broadcasters such as Al Jazeera, The Guardian, BBC and Foreign Policy. When she's not reporting on war & conflict or environmental issues, she's a regular volunteer with SkatePal, and has shared a recipe for one of the heartiest breakfasts out there – Ful Medames (PREVIOUS PAGE). It's a dish shared across many Arab nations, each bringing their own tweaks, however this one has been crafted to perfection through her time spent in Ramallah.

Josh Sutton is a skater, father and foodie from England. As a veteran food-writer, he's published recipes in various magazines, but as a newbie skateboarder, he picked up a board only recently – at age 51 – to learn with his son. With a passion for food, a love of the Arabic language and an enthusiasm for skateboarding, Josh got involved with SkatePal in 2018. The simple salad recipe (FOLLOWING PAGE) is donated from 'Cookpal'; a project he undertook to raise money for SkatePal, in which he created a selection of recipes inspired by his time in the Palestinian West Bank.

Tessa Fox introduces a group of siblings to their first flatbank, and all the potential joy that a simple concrete incline can hold.
PHOTO BY TOM BIRD.

Fennel &

Radish Salad

– by JOSH SUTTON

- **1–2 HANDFULS FRESH WATERCRESS**
- **10-12 RADISHES** (THINLY SLICED)
- **1 BULB FENNEL** (SLICED)
- **100g BLOCK FETA** (CUBED)
- **1 LIME** (JUICED)
- **FEW GLUGS OF OLIVE OIL**
- **SALT & PEPPER**

SERVES: **5–6**
PREP TIME: **15 MINS**

This one goes out to even the most kitchen-illiterate skaters out there...

1. Prepare all the ingredients and place everything into a big bowl.

2. Pour over the lime juice, season with salt & pepper and toss together. Transfer to a serving dish and drizzle over some good quality olive oil (when it comes to salads, don't scrimp on the quality of the oil).

3. Admire yourself for being so nutritious.

[LEFT] **DIY adjustable hippie jump bar. Asira Al-Shamaliya skatepark, 2017.** PHOTO BY JULIAN MAEHRLEIN.

[RIGHT] **Zaina Amous learning ride-on grinds for the first time. Ramallah, 2018.** PHOTO BY BEN BRAVENEC.

Hummus

– by MOATH QASHOO (BAQA AL-HATAB / LONDON)
مُعاذ قشوع

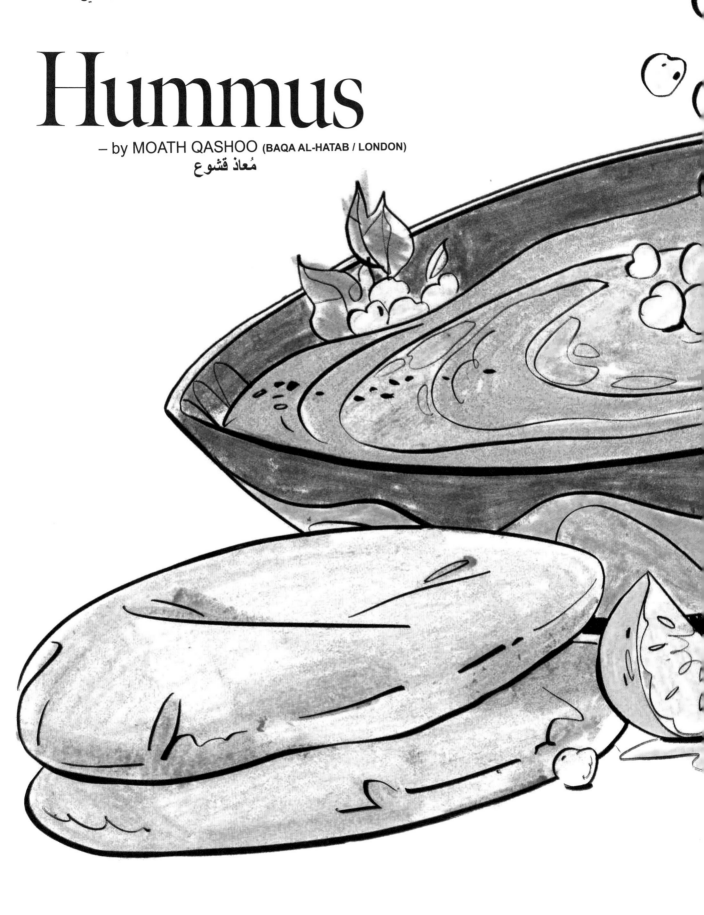

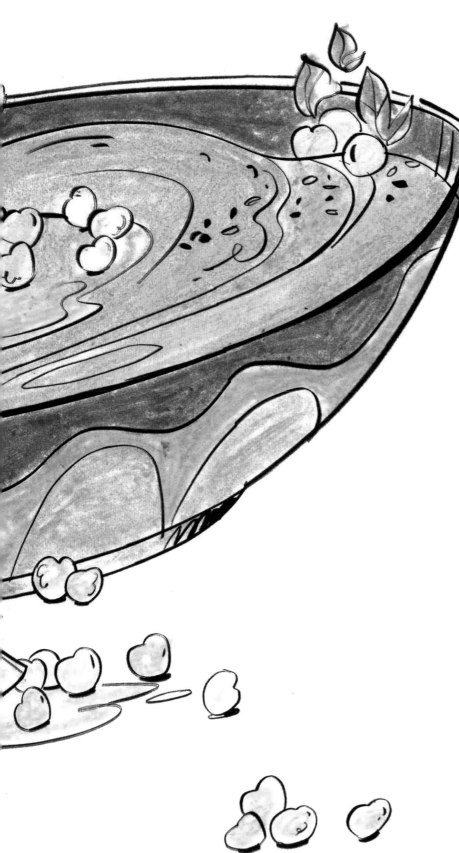

Where to begin with the humble hummus?

A dish as old as Palestine itself. So old, in fact, that Arab nations have even tired of debating who invented it. Is it a dip or a dish? That's contentious. What can be agreed upon, however, are two things: one, that the word 'hummus' is Arabic for chickpea, and two, that hummus goes with anything at any time. Bread, vegetables, falafel? Breakfast, lunch, dinner? The answer is always "yes". And as a good source of protein and fibre, everybody wins. Even vegans.

This recipe comes courtesy of the Qashoo family, originally from Baqa Al-Hatab in the West Bank, but now residing in the UK and running 'Hiba Express' – a series of restaurants that seek to bring a taste of Palestine to the heart of London. After a two-hour game of frisbee on a rainy Sunday, Moath Qahsoo finally relented and shared his family recipe for this Middle-Eastern gem.

Moath Qashoo مُعاذ قشوع runs the London-based Hiba – *meaning 'lovely surprise' in Arabic* – alongside his wife Nada who hails from the scenic Palestinian village of Akka. Since visiting the SkatePal-built skatepark in nearby Asira Al-Shamaliya before relocating to London, Moath and the Qashoo family have become huge supporters of our programme. In fact, they're responsible for the delicious falafel found on the underside of the SkatePal x Isle deck (NEXT PAGE). Go check them out, and say we sent ya! (FIND THEIR ADDRESS AT THE BACK OF THIS BOOK).

Moath & Nada take a break from serving the steady flow of customers at Mini Hiba to grant us a family portrait.
PHOTO BY DOROTHY ISKRZYNSKA.

- 500g **DRIED CHICKPEAS**
  (SOAKED 24HRS)
- 1 TBSP **BAKING SODA**
- 6 TBSP **TAHINI**
- 2 CLOVES **GARLIC**
- 5 TBSP **OLIVE OIL**
- 2 **LEMONS** (JUICED)
- 3 TSP **SALT**
- 1 FRESH **GREEN CHILLI**
  (FINELY SLICED)
- 1 **BELL PEPPER** (CHOPPED)
- 1 TBSP **SUMAC**
- 1 CUP **FRESH PARSLEY**
  (CHOPPED)

SERVES: **4 – 8**
PREP TIME: **3 HRS**
(+24 HRS TO SOAK CHICKPEAS)

1.   Before getting started, you must soak the dried chickpeas in twice their volume of cold water for 24hrs. If possible, rinse and change the water every few hours. Moath recommends 8 times (!!) throughout the process, but it's not a dealbreaker.

2.   After 24 hrs of soaking, add 1 tablespoon of baking soda to the water, then bring to a simmer over the stove for 2.5 hrs.

3.   Once cooked, drain the chickpeas – saving a cup of cooking water – and transfer them to a blender. Blitz into a creamy texture, adding a drop of the cooking water to loosen up the mixture if it's too coarse. **Don't forget to save a handful of chickpeas for the dressing!**

4.   Once the desired texture is reached, add 3-4 ice cubes, blitz once more then allow to cool. If you want to go the extra mile, using some of the chickpea water to make ice cubes will make this extra special!

5.   Once cooled, add the tahini, olive oil, salt, garlic and lemon to the mixture, then blitz once more in the blender to combine.

6.   For the dressing, add the handful of whole chickpeas you saved earlier to a bowl, and combine with the chilli pepper, bell pepper, lemon juice, pepper, sumac and fresh parsley.

7.   To serve, scoop a few big dollops of hummus into a shallow bowl. Using the back of a spoon, make a well in the middle, add a spoonful of your dressing, then pour over olive oil making a small swimming pool. Serve immediately with an extra sprinkle of parsley.

Moath recommends blending the chickpeas before adding the other ingredients, as it is important to helps keep the consistency of the dish. If your hummus is starting to dry out, just refresh it with some more olive oil and you're good to go!

!!! **CHICKPEA WARNING** !!!
HUMMUS SHOULD ONLY REALLY BE ATTEMPTED WITH A FOOD PROCESSOR. YOU CAN TAKE A CHANCE ON WORKING YOUR BICEPS WITH A MASHER, BUT IT'LL TAKE HOURS AND THE CONSISTENCY WILL BE FAR FROM IDEAL.

Nick Jensen puts the final touches to the artwork for the Isle x SkatePal collaboration graphic – part of their 'Curiousities' deck series. PHOTO BY SAM ASHLEY.

Falafel

– by ABOOD BARHAN (ASIRA AL-SHAMALIYA)
عبود برهان

A tiresome, 20 minute uphill walk separates the SkatePal apartment and Abood's falafel place. Yet over the last few years this has done little to stop volunteers from summoning their last bit of energy after the evening session and climbing the hill to reach what has become one of SkatePal's premiere food joints. Although nothing on the exterior indicates that it's anything other than someone's home, the legendary status of Abood's restaurant is passed on through the changing feet of volunteers each year. Once inside, however, there are plenty of clues to signal you're in the right place: a used deck sitting atop the aging deep-fat fryer or lunatic cats running around in the backyard. According to Izzeldin [Bukhari], *"We eat falafel all over the West Bank, like it's part of Arab identity... but trace it back far enough and you end up at Egypt's Coptic Christians"*. Regardless of its origins, food doesn't last from early Biblical times through to the present day unless it tastes f**king good.

Only God knows how many crispy falafels have emerged from Abood's deep fat fryer over the years. Abood definitely doesn't know. A gift from past SkatePal volunteers still sits proudly above it. PHOTOS BY TOM BIRD.

According to <u>Abood</u> عبود برهان the doors to his
opened in 1992. Originally run by his Father,
still prepares the batches of falafel mix in the morni
began helping out from age fourteen. Given the
falafel in Palestine, we worried that Abood's reci
a family secret, guarded under lock-and-key. B
floated the idea for this recipe with him, he simp

– **1kg DRIED CHICKPEAS**
(SOAKED 24HRS)
– **1 BUNCH PARSLEY**
(STALKS REMOVED)
– **1/4 BUNCH CORIANDER**
(STALKS REMOVED)
– **2 LARGE WHITE ONIONS**
(ROUGHLY CHOPPED)
– **4 CLOVES GARLIC**
– **2-4 BIRDS EYE CHILLIES**
(OPTIONAL)
– **1 TSP CAYENNE** (GROUND)
– **1 TSP CUMIN** (GROUND)
– **1 TSP NUTMEG**
– **1 TSP SESAME SEEDS**
– **1/2 TSP BAKING POWDER**
– **2-3 TSP SALT**
– **500ml SUNFLOWER OIL**
– **5 RIPE TOMATOES** (DICED)
– **1 CUCUMBER** (DICED)
– **FRESH PITTAS**

SERVES: **8-10**
PREP TIME: **45 MINS**
(+24 HRS TO SOAK CHICKPEAS)

!!! <u>**CHICKPEA WARNING**</u> !!!
FALAFEL SHOULD ONLY REALLY BE ATTEMPTED WITH A FOOD PROCESSOR. YOU CAN TAKE A CHANCE ON WORKING YOUR BICEPS WITH A MASHER, BUT IT'LL TAKE HOURS AND THE CONSISTENCY WILL BE FAR FROM IDEAL.

1. Pour the dried chickpeas into a big bowl. Pour over cold water (twice the volume of the chickpeas). Add a tsp of salt, and leave to soak for approx 24 hours. Change the water a couple of times throughout the day if possible, then go to bed dreaming of fluffy falafel pieces.

The next day...

2. Drain the chickpeas and add to a big bowl. Remove the stalks from the parsley and the coriander, so you're just left with the leaves. If it's a Sunday and you've got heaps of time, feel free to pick the leaves – otherwise just bunch together and remove the stalks with a knife, then add the leaves to the big bowl.

3. Roughly chop the onions and remove the garlic cloves from their skins, then add to the same big bowl. Mix together, then add to the blender and start blitzing (you'll probably have to do this in batches).

4. Abood says that you can dice up 2-4 birds eye chillies and add them to the chickpea mix (removing the seeds for less spice) – however he makes a killer chilli sauce to accompany, so prefers to omit them here.

5. Once blended into an even consistency, decant into a big bowl and combine with the sesame seeds, cayenne pepper, cumin, nutmeg, baking powder, salt and 3 tablespoons of water. The ideal consistency should be like clumpy sand. If the mixture's a little dry, simply add another teaspoon of water, mix and repeat until it feels right.

6. Fill a small saucepan with a few inches of sunflower oil, and place over a medium heat. Meanwhile, begin shaping clumps of the mixture into little discs (thin 52mm wheels are a good size reference). Once the oil is spitting and angry (necessary conditions for the crispiest falafel) you can begin plopping in the pieces, cooking until golden. Remember to place them on a paper towel once removed to soak up excess oil.

7. Throw your pitta onto an open flame and turn so the edges crisp up and it starts to inflate. Remove, slice open, spread inside a dash of hummus (see Moath Qashoo's recipe), followed by 3-4 falafel pieces and crush slightly. Top with diced fresh tomato, cucumber and some chilli sauce.

Abood Barhan, of the famed 'Abood's falafel', takes a break from the kitchen. 2019. PHOTO BY TOM BIRD.

FALAFEL

Friday sessions at the skatepark often end up running around after enthusiastic young skaters, shouting 'kha-las!'(finished) whilst trying to pack away the equipment. But once the day is over, there's no better sight than this. PHOTO BY TOMAS PAJDLHAUSER.

About to take the plunge. Asira Al-Shamaliya, 2016. PHOTO BY OWEN GODBERT.

Q&A	

Aram Sabbah آرام صباح

AND

Wala Qamhieh ولاء قمحيه

On SkatePal's journey to implement a self-sustaining skate scene that relies less on international support, we are focusing on employing local staff and training local volunteers to gradually take over the projects and programmes. Leading this are local skaters Aram Sabbah and Wala Qamhieh. We spoke with both of them about the current skate scene and their hopes for the future.

"It's important for any kid growing up in Palestine to have something that takes their mind off some of the shitty things that happen here."

SkatePal: **Aram – you've been part of SkatePal since the very beginning. Can you explain a little bit about how you initially became involved in the project, and what your role is within SkatePal now?**

Aram Sabbah: The first time I got involved with SkatePal was in 2013, when Charlie had just finished building the mini ramp at the Sharek Youth Forum in Ramallah. My friend Adham and I had heard about the ramp so we went to check it out. We met Charlie and his brother Jack, introduced ourselves and asked if they needed help with anything – which ended up just helping teach some of the kids during the summer. Fast forward 7 years and I now work full-time as a Local Manager for SkatePal, being the on-the-ground contact for everything in Palestine, e.g. arranging volunteer accommodation, recycling and reshaping old boards for the kids etc. In general my role is to shred and help everyone else to shred (laughs).

For anyone reading who might have never stepped on a skateboard, can you explain what it means to you, and why young people in Palestine are getting involved?

AS: Skateboarding is something that gives your soul a way to express itself. It's a feeling that nothing matters except the fact you're riding a board with four wheels and enjoying the company of your friends riding with you. It's important for any kid growing up in Palestine to have something that takes their mind off some of the shitty things that happen here. For some kids, it's a way to channel their frustrations, for others, it's just hardcore skateboarding.

Wala – as a more recent addition to the SkatePal family, can you tell us about how you got involved?

Wala Quamhieh: After spending two years in France completing my masters (and also being introduced to skateboarding), I arrived back in Palestine in late 2018 hoping to find a place where I would be able to skate without people staring at me. I had a friend whose son was also interested in skateboarding, and she'd heard about a skatepark just outside of my hometown of Nablus, so she suggested we go there and explore. There we met a nice group of SkatePal volunteers, and for the next month I spent a lot of time with them – skating, sharing meals and even celebrating dia de los muertos (day of the dead) together.

I continued going to the skatepark after the volunteer programme had ended, and the following year began assisting as a translator between the kids and the volunteers. This is where it all started, the volunteers put me in touch with Charlie and I started volunteering officially. As my skating progressed, I began to help with teaching – especially during the girls-only sessions – and helping volunteers liaise with the local community to organise events, like the skate film screening in the village.

[PREVIOUS LEFT] **Aram leading the way and making footsteps for a whole generation to follow. Ramallah, 2019.** PHOTO BY JOHNNY MCMULLAN.

[PREVIOUS RIGHT] **Wala Qamhieh. Asira Al-Shamaliya, 2019.** PHOTO BY ANIL ILTAS.

Wala, Aram and other local skaters take part in the first board recycling workshop hosted by Re:ply: learning how planing and sanding techniques can be used to upcycle old skateboards. Ramallah, 2019. PHOTOS BY PAULA GRANT.

Danny from Re:ply helping local skaters sketch out ideas for their new recycled boards.
Ramallah, 2019. PHOTO BY PAULA GRANT.

Recently SkatePal have been running skateboard recycling workshops across Palestine in partnership with Re:ply Skateboards and our local volunteers. How did they go?

WQ: I saw a picture on Instagram of an old skateboard Aram had recycled with Re:ply. His work was super neat and I thought: I want to try this too!

A few days later, SkatePal organised a workshop in Ramallah for anyone in the community that was interested, so of course, I joined immediately! The workshop taught us how to use a selection of tools – many I'd never seen before in my life! It was such a nice atmosphere, and everyone was so friendly and really enthusiastic about the first skateboard I recycled, which motivated me even more to be a part of this.

The following day, we took the workshop to Asira Al-Shamaliya, where a lot of the kids (many too young to handle tools) were able to become part of the process by making graphics for the newly upcycled decks using paints and pens. It's so nice to have something other than the skateboarding itself that everyone in the community can contribute to and feel proud of.

As well as the community benefit, there's also a logistical benefit to recycling old boards, as there is currently nowhere to buy skateboard equipment in Palestine.

AS: Yeah, we don't have any way of importing skateboards into Palestine. There are skateboard supply shops in Israel, but that's obviously not an option for the majority of Palestinians who're forbidden from crossing the separation barrier. Right now, the supply chain of equipment is mostly via volunteers bringing over donated equipment, but recycling old skateboards gives us a new way of providing boards for the kids who want to shred. I hope that through the workshops, kids can continue to learn to reshape and recycle their boards so they can maintain their progress in skateboarding.

WQ: And save the planet! It's a pretty cool way to get people to think about sustainability too.

It seems like the community of skateboarders around Palestine are becoming more interconnected. What started as young people from the same communities meeting and bonding at a skatepark in their area, has now grown into skaters from all over Palestine connecting with each other through online social platforms…

AS: Yeah, skateboarders all over the country are taking big steps in connecting with each other on social media and hitting up each other to go out and have a skate session. It's really beautiful to see them growing up and being passionate about something that connects them, even outside of the skate classes. Many are skating almost everyday by themselves now, which for me, means that we are on the right path in creating a skate scene that sustains itself without international help.

"It's so nice to have something other than the skateboarding itself that everyone in the community can contribute to and feel proud of."

Aram, hippie jump at Qadura Park – as seen in Thrasher magazine. Ramallah, 2020. PHOTO BY CLEMENT LE GALL.

A lot of skateboarders would agree that it gives you a reason to explore – whether to connect with other skaters or discover new spots. It seems that Palestine's public skateparks like Asira and Jayyous now provide a reason for young people to travel (when possible*) to parts of Palestine that they would have previously never had a reason to visit. What are your thoughts on this?

AS: It's true! Skateboarding has definitely given a reason to go out and visit places that they would never usually think about visiting or care to see. Definitely having skateparks and new skate-spots spread across the country is opening the eyes of some kids. Exploring new places at a young age is critical to growing and having your own perspective on the life that you lead – especially here in Palestine.

*For clarification, maybe you can expand on why I say 'when possible' in the above question?

WQ: Even within the West Bank, the military impose lots of travel restrictions. This means that on some days I can go to Jayyous without any issues, and other days, for no reason, I cannot. The village is closed. It's close to the separation wall, and tensions are often high in these villages because the occupation is so painfully clear. Even peaceful protests can suddenly turn nasty and of course this makes our parents worry, so most young Palestinians are not used to exploring new places on their own.

"It's really beautiful to see them growing up and being passionate about something that connects them, even outside of the skate classes."

Looking back to when SkatePal's first project took shape in 2013, what are you most proud of in the journey so far, and what role do you think SkatePal can play for Palestinian communities in the future?

AS: There are so many things that I'm proud of. We have been helping others to grow and growing ourselves in the process. It has been a blessing for me to be involved and it's the main reason that I didn't dip out of the country to seek a better life elsewhere. I'm excited to see what the future holds for all of us!

WQ: I'm definitely happy to see Palestinian girls being accepted as part of the skating community, which would typically be taboo. For example, I grew up wanting to ride a bike, but that was not possible for women in Palestine (even today), however I've found myself having all the confidence in the world to skate around my city with a bunch of local and foreign skaters.

And as this is a cookbook – what's the one food that everyone should try if they visit the West Bank?

AS: Okay okay! Best thing is to try to get yourself an invite to someone's house (which is really easy in Palestine because of the warm hospitality we have) and ask them to make you Malfouf (my favourite Palestinian dish) or Musakhan or Maqlouba and if you're vegetarian or vegan ask for Mlokheye or Mujadara.

CLOCKWISE FROM LEFT: Omar, Aram, Wala, Osama, Sireen, Karim & Mohammed, Ali, Ryan, Lara, Asinat, Jehad, Ledia, Noha & Mary. Asira Al-Shamaliya, 2019. PHOTO BY CLEMENT LE GALL.

The quiet before the storm. SkatePal's free-to-use starter boards, collected and transported to the West Bank by various international volunteers, await the after-school frenzy. PHOTO BY TOM BIRD.

HOW TO MAKE YOUR OWN DIY CHOPPING BOARD

Some decks are beyond refurbishment. And yes, snapping your board sucks. But on the bright side, there are many other uses for old skateboards – like a handy portable chopping board for those summer BBQ sessions at your local skatepark. Here are some instructions on how to prepare one for yourself...

STEP 1 – Get out there and have some fun.

STEP 2 – Not everyone is blessed as a truckbolt warrior. If disaster strikes, don't fret. It might end your session, but it's just the start of dinner.

STEP 3 – Take the larger piece of the broken board and remove the grip tape to reveal a nice, smooth surface. The easiest way is to use a craft knife to peel back the edge, and a hairdryer to loosen the adhesive enough to remove it completely. Finally, scrub off any residue with hot soapy water.

STEP 4 – There you have it, a brand new chopping board! (Of course the concave of the deck will cause stability issues, but these can be corrected by simply using a plane saw to shave off a layer of the underside). Enjoy!

"Here's one we prepared earlier". For the first few years of the programme, the SkatePal kitchen was equipped with a revolving selection of snapped-decks-turned-chopping-boards. 2016. PHOTO BY TOM BIRD.

D.I.Y. CHOPPING BOARD

Hemp Seed Tabboula

– by IZZELDIN BUKHARI, FOUNDER OF SACRED CUISINE

عزدين بوخاري

(JERUSALEM)

So you've rolled your ankle for the fifth time this week?

Bummer, it happens. The good news is that tabboula is not only a speedy dish to make, but this particular recipe has been designed to give you a speedy recovery too.

Tabboula is one of the most famous salads from the Levant. Typically made with bulgur or couscous, Izzeldin has put a twist on tradition specifically for this book, focusing on ingredients with a high calcium content and anti-inflammatory properties, making this the perfect dish if you're nursing an injury.

Izzeldin discovered skateboarding after moving to the United States for university, and having grown up in one of the oldest Sufi families in East Jerusalem, food has always played an important role in his life – particularly through the practice of 'langar', a rich Sufi tradition where food is provided to those less fortunate. As a keen skateboarder whose food pop-up – Sacred Cuisine – hosts regular events across Palestine, he's perfectly placed to share his wisdom with us…

HEMP SEED TABBOULA

Since moving back to Jerusalem from the United States, and observing how the military occupation of the West Bank is increasingly cutting the ties Palestinian people once had to their land, <u>Izzeldin Bukhari</u> عزدين بوخاري founded Sacred Cuisine as an attempt to preserve the rich history of Palestinian cooking. He runs a series of innovative food related pop-ups for both Palestinians & Israelis on either side of the separation wall, seeking to educate, inspire and connect these communities through food.

Izzeldin Bukhari, Jerusalem, 2019. PHOTO BY DIANA MUSA.

- 150g HULLED HEMP SEEDS
- 100g ARUGULA / ROCKET
  (WASHED AND CHOPPED)
- 1 LARGE AVOCADO (CUBED)
- 2 CUCUMBERS
  (DICED AND DESEEDED)
- 1 TBSP FLAX SEEDS
- SEEDS OF 1 LARGE
  POMEGRANATE
- 1 LARGE LEMON (JUICED)
- 2 TBSP OF OLIVE OIL
- 1 TBSP OF HEMP OIL (OPTIONAL)
- 1 TBSP OF SUMAC
- SALT & PEPPER

1.   Put the hemp seeds in a big bowl and add the olive oil, hemp oil (if you have it) and the lemon juice. Leave to marinade for around 15 mins.

2.   Add the arugula, cucumbers and pomegranate seeds, mix well, then add the avocado, and season with salt and pepper. Turn over gently so that the avocado chunks don't turn to mush, then taste and add more seasoning if necessary,

3.   Transfer to a bowl and garnish with the flax seeds and sumac. Saahha!

SERVES: 2
PREP TIME: 30 MINS

"Hemp seeds are high in proteins that are essential for muscles and joints. Avocados are full of healthy fats, which increase the absorption of the nutrients. Arugula can help improve muscle oxygenation during exercise. Flax seeds are high in good calories. And pomegranate is full of antioxidants that are famous for anti-inflammatory properties."

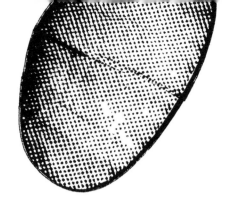

"People think I'm creating something new, but I'm actually just digging into the past".

IZZELDIN BUKHARI

Mohammad (pictured) — one of two brothers that runs this Nablus bakery — prepares 'tamreyah', as their late father looks down from the picture frame, keeping a watchful eye that his sons are staying true to the family recipe. Nablus Old City, 2019. PHOTO BY TOM BIRD.

HEMP SEED TABBOULA

Pomegranates. They become a lot more tasty once you learn how to properly deseed them.
Ramallah, 2019. PHOTO BY TOM BIRD.

Yoga Instructor, Majdal Soban, works with Izzeldin on a series of events called 'Mindful Eating', which seek to discover the connection between food and spirituality, and how it impacts our minds and bodies. For each event, they develop a special menu and a yoga sequence based around a particular theme.

For this book, Majdal has shared a simple sequence to help skaters restore energy, rejuvenate, and release physical and mental tensions to help balance both sides of the body. She also emphasises that we should view the following as 'innercise' as much as exercise, helping us to explore the interconnected nature of our body and mind – an essential element of skateboarding.

Majdal in Jerusalem. PHOTO BY AHMED IDEA.

1. VIPARITA KARANI

Sit beside a wall, lie on your back, raise your l
and swing your hips round, resting your heels against the wall. Bring yo
as close to the wall as possible, so that the back of your legs are flat ag
and your body is at a 90° angle. Hold for 5-10 minutes. This pose helps
blood flow, alleviating fluids in the feet and legs that tend to stagnate fo
a skate session.

4. MARJAIASANA

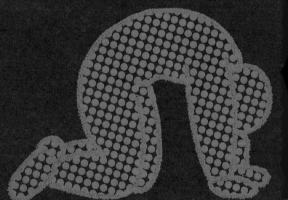

Get onto all fours, ensuring that your wrists, shoulders, knees
are all aligned. Inhale deeply, dropping your belly toward the floor and
your spine upwards. Raise your chin up as high as possible. Hold f
seconds. Exhale and drop your chin down towards your chest, allow
back to arch the other way. Keep your elbows locked through the mo
Repeat for 5-10 rounds of breath. This pose improves posture, bala

2. APANASANA

Lying on your back and with your head resting on the floor, inhale deeply. As you exhale, bring your knees towards your chest and pull them close with your arms. Hold for 2-3 minutes. To further elongate your spine, you can draw your forehead in towards your knees. Allowing your knees to rock gently from side to side will help relieve tension from your lower back. This pose eases digestion, relieves stomach cramps and improves blood circulation.

3. SUPTA KAPOTASANA

Lie on your back, with your knees bent and both feet on the floor. Raise one foot and rest it on the opposite leg, with your ankle just below the knee. Push the raised knee away from you until you feel the stretch in your inner thigh. Release, then thread your hands through your legs, clasping them behind the thigh and pulling your knee towards your chest. Repeat on both legs, holding for 2–5 minutes each. This pose relieves tension across the hips, back and butt.

5. ADHO MUKHA SVANASANA

From the all fours position, push your toes into the floor, forcing your hips upward to create an 'A' shape with your body. Try to avoid letting your shoulders hunch towards your ears. Spread your fingers for stability and keep your neck, back and arms all in one line. Push down through your heels, feeling the stretch down the back of your legs. Hold for 5 deep inhales. This pose relieves tension in legs and spine, and helps energize the body and improve concentration.

6. TADASANA

Stand with your feet hip-width apart. Ground your weight evenly across all four corners of both feet and raise your arches. Bring your body into alignment – centering your torso above your hips, rolling your shoulders back and allowing your ribcage to lengthen. Elongate your neck, draw your chin up, and evenly space your arms from your hips, opening your fingers wide. Inhale and exhale deeply. This subtle pose is great for improving posture and focusing on your breath.

Ismael from Jayyous takes his first tentative steps on a skateboard during the intial months following our completion of the skatepark there, just a short drive from the city of Qalqilya. 2017. PHOTO BY EMIL AGERSKOV.

Aubergine, pepper & chickpea stew

– by WHAT THE FATTOUSH

So much more than the sum of its parts, this is a warm, comforting, super filling yet healthy dish that everyone seems to love. It sits somewhere between a Turkish 'Imam bayildi' and a Lebanese 'Maghmour' and can be eaten on its own, with rice, used as a base for shakshuka or on top of toasted pitta chips with fresh herbs as a fatteh.

AUBERGINE STEW

<u>What The Fattoush </u>is a pop-up kitchen in the U.K., run by Jess Howe and Megan Maule, specialising in plant-based cuisine with a Middle Eastern influence. The pair met whilst working for a humanitarian organisation in Calais, France, preparing food at one of the shelters built to aid refugees and those seeking asylum. It was here, working and interacting across a spectrum of Arab nationalities, that they became immersed in the cooking and culture. Following trips to Palestine, they decided to start a project together that combined cuisine with a cause. Since starting in 2017, they've provided food at various SkatePal fundraising events, and continue to donate 10% of their proceeds towards our work. Cheers guys!

- **4 AUBERGINES**
  (CUBED – approx 2cm)
- **150ML OLIVE OIL**
- **1 ONION** (DICED)
- **2 RED PEPPERS** (DICED)
- **4 GARLIC CLOVES**
  (FINELY CHOPPED)
- **2 TSP CUMIN** (GROUND)
- **1.5 TSP PAPRIKA** (GROUND)
- **2 TINS OF TOMATOES**
- **1 TSP CASTER SUGAR**
- **2 TSP DRIED OREGANO**
- **1 TIN OF CHICKPEAS**
- **SALT & PEPPER**

SERVES: **6**
PREP TIME: **1 HR**

1.　Heat the oil on a medium to high heat in a large frying pan and add the aubergines. Cook until brown on each side.

2.　Once the aubergines are cooked through, remove them and set aside for later. Using the same pan, reduce the heat and fry the onions and peppers until they're soft (approximately 10 minutes).

3.　Add the garlic, cumin and paprika and cook for a further minute.

4.　Once the garlic becomes fragrant, add the fried aubergines and cook down until a paste–like mixture is formed.

5.　Add the tinned tomatoes, chickpeas, sugar, oregano, half a tin of water, salt and pepper and cook on a low heat for about 45 minutes. The longer you cook the stew, the better it's going to taste!

What The Fattoush recommend leaving it overnight if you want maximum flavour, since most stews taste better the next day. And if you make too much, this dish also doubles as a great base layer for a breakfast shakshuka!

[LEFT] **Jessica Howe and Megan Maule, a.k.a. What The Fattoush. London, 2019.** PHOTO BY TOM BIRD.

[RIGHT] **Jess & Meg taking care of the hungry crowds during SkatePal's annual fundraiser jam at London's Gillet Square.**

AUBERGINE STEW

Malfouf

— by ARAM & SORIDA SABBAH (RAMALLAH)

آرام و سريدا صبّاح

When asked which food he most craves when away from home, Aram didn't hesitate for a second.

"Malfouf! We gotta make it, but I gotta check when my mother is free 'cause I don't know what I'm doing…"

No matter where you go in the world, some things remain the same. Food is comfort and comfort is home. And so we found ourselves in the family home of Aram (SkatePal's local manager) and his mother Sorida, born and raised in Columbia,

but to Palestinian parents who ensured she understood her roots – which of course means learning how to prepare malfouf.

Here, in their cosy Ramallah home, a mix of SkatePal volunteers, Aram's school-friends, and a couple of other visiting skaters gathered around a large plate piled high with tightly wrapped cabbage leaves filled with spiced meat and rice. Malfouf is similar to stuffed grape leaves, commonly know as 'dolmas' or 'warak enab' in the Arab world, yet Aram assures us there is no comparison. Nothing draws him more towards his home country than the prospect of his mother's home-cooked malfouf. So here it is…

Since graduating from university in Tunisia, <u>Aram Sabbah</u> آرام صبّاح moved back to Ramallah in 2019 and took on the role of SkatePal's Local Manager, having been part of the family since day one. Originally from Jenin, a city in the north of the West Bank, Aram was first introduced to skateboarding in 2012 and has since become a pillar of Palestine's skate community. In 2019, Aram was invited to take part in the 'Globally Stoked' panel discussion at Pushing Boarders skateboarding conference in Malmö, Sweden, to discuss the impact of international skate-NGOs on local communities around the world.

- 750g MINCED BEEF
- 500g OF WHITE RICE
- 4 WHITE CABBAGES
- 12 GARLIC CLOVES (PEELED)
- 2 TBSP CUMIN (GROUND)
- 1 TBSP CINNAMON (GROUND)
- 1 TBSP CARDAMOM (GROUND)
- 1 TBSP NUTMEG (GROUND)
- 1L NATURAL YOGHURT
- SALT & PEPPER

SERVES: **4**
PREP TIME: **1 HR**

1.	Cover the rice with boiling water and allow to stand for 15–20 mins. It doesn't need to cook fully – as we'll be cooking it later in the process.

2.	Fill a large saucepan with water and bring to a simmer. One-by-one (depending on the size of your spot) place the cabbages in the water and cook for 5 minutes, turning occasionally until the outer leaves are softened and translucent (but not like a wet tissue).

3.	Using tongs lift the cabbage out of the water, let the majority of the water drip back into the pot (don't turn the hob off), before placing onto a chopping board until cool enough to handle.

4.	Carefully remove the cooked leaves and put to one side. Place the cabbage back into the water to cook the next layer of leaves, turning occasionally. Repeat this process until just the stalk is left. This takes a while but it's totally worth it!

5.	After the rice has stood for 15-20 minutes, drain using a sieve, then rinse with cold water for a minute just to clean it. Combine it with the raw minced meat and spices. Season with salt and pepper and mix together using your hands.

6.	Now to pull everything together. One by one, arrange a small line of the rice mixture inside a leaf and roll, sealing the edges, burrito style. For those of you who smoke roll-ups, this is your time to shine.

****Sorida recommends keeping the veins of the leaf horizontal when rolling –
it'll make your life easier – and don't forget the rice will expand again when
it cooks, so don't overfill them!****

7.	When all the cabbage leaves are rolled, place them back into the same pot that you used to separate the leaves. Stack them layer by layer, adding 3–4 peeled cloves of garlic to each layer. Use any over-cooked leaves that couldn't be used for rolling to cover the cabbage 'cigars'. Refill the pot with the water you used to cook the cabbage, return the pot to the boil, and place a lid on the top. Cook for around 15-20 mins, topping up with water if necessary.

8.	Once the cigars are feeling firm, the meat should be cooked through and ready to eat. Drain any remaining water and tip the steaming cigars onto a plate. Separate the natural yogurt between a few dishes, and serve with freshly toasted pitta.

[LEFT] **SkatePal's local manager, Aram Sabbah, and
his mum Sorida on the balcony of their family home.
Ramallah, 2019.**

[RIGHT] **This gives you an idea of what Step 7 in the
recipe should look like, followed by Step 8, as proudly
demonstrated by Aram.** PHOTOS BY TOM BIRD.

Aram Sabbah putting in the work on a wallie at Ramallah Youth Centre. 2019. PHOTO BY TOMAS PAJDLHAUSER.

Fattet Makdous

— by SAMI TAMIMI
(JERUSALEM / LONDON)

'Fattet' or 'fattah' originated in Syria or Belad Al Sham, but has become a dish widely loved across the Middle East.

"That means it's one of these dishes that doesn't just vary between countries, but even between households", admits Sami.

Sami Tamimi – internationally known as one of the founding partners of the Ottolenghi chain and for his contributions to their best selling cookbook series – was born and raised in the cobbled streets of East Jerusalem. It was here that he remembers being frequently exposed to this dish – particularly a vegetarian version – even though it's more commonly made with chicken or minced meat.

After co-authoring the best selling cookbook 'Jerusalem' (2012), Tamimi released 'Falastin' (2019) – a more personal and nuanced exploration of his native cuisine. As a patron of SkatePal's work, we thought

we'd chance our luck by asking him for a recipe – and were honoured when he suggested creating one especially for this book! We'll hand over the mic to the man himself…

"Hearty, humble, healthy and utterly delicious. The different layers of flavour in this Fattet work so well together; with a crunchy layer of pita bread, topped with meaty roast aubergine, sweet-sour tomato sauce and the creamy yogurt tahini sauce. All topped with buttery almonds, parsley, chilli, pomegranate seeds and served with a big bowl of freshly chopped salad and small plates of crunchy pickles – this dish is built to be shared among friends and family."

So next time there's a jam at your local skatepark, keep this one in mind!

Sami Tamimi is an internationally acclaimed Palestinian chef, who cut his teeth at restaurants in his home city of Jerusalem, before perfecting his craft around the world. After settling in London, he and Yotam Ottolenghi met whilst working between the deli and kitchen at the same restaurant. In 2002 they partnered up, along with Noam Bar, and set up the now famous Ottolenghi company, where Sami works as executive head chef across their restaurants developing cutting-edge menus by infusing his deep knowledge of Middle Eastern cuisine.

Sami Tamimi, London. PHOTO BY KEIKO OIKAWA.

– 2 PITA BREAD OR TORTILLA (CUT INTO 3CM PIECES)
– 2 AUBERGINE, APPROX 500g (CHOPPED INTO 3CM CUBES)
– 8 TBSP OLIVE OIL
– 1 MEDIUM ONION (DICED)
– 1 GARLIC CLOVE (DICED)
– 2 FRESH CHILLIES (1 GREEN, 1 RED, BOTH FINELY CHOPPED)
– 1 LEMON (JUICED)
– 2 TSP SUMAC
– ½ TSP SWEET PAPRIKA
– 3 TBSP TAHINI
– 450g PASSATA
– 400g GREEK YOGHURT
– 1 TBSP POMEGRANATE MOLASSES
– 30g POMEGRANATE SEEDS (OPTIONAL)
– 45g ALMONDS (BLANCHED & TOASTED – SEE RECIPE)
– 1 TSP BUTTER
– 1 HANDFUL OF PARSLEY (ROUGHLY CHOPPED)
– SALT & PEPPER

SERVES: **4**
PREP TIME: **1 HR**

1.   Pre-heat the oven to 180C. Place the bread pieces in a bowl with 3 tablespoons of olive oil and mix well to coat. Lay the bread in one layer into a baking sheet and bake until golden and crispy – approximately 15 minutes. Set aside for later.

2.   Turn up the oven to 230C. Place the aubergine chunks in a large bowl, add 3 tablespoons of olive oil, the sumac, paprika and a good pinch of salt and grind of black pepper, then toss well to coat. Arrange the aubergine pieces flat on a baking sheet and roast until golden and cooked through – approximately 20 minutes.

3.   While the aubergine is cooking, make the yoghurt sauce. Place the Greek yoghurt, tahini, garlic, green chilli, two tablespoons of lemon juice and a large pinch of salt in a bowl, and mix well to combine. Store in the fridge to cool.

4.   Now for the tomato sauce. In a small saucepan, heat two tablespoons of olive oil, add the onion and cook on a medium-low heat for around 10 minutes or until it's golden and soft. Add the tomato passata, pomegranate molasses, a pinch of salt and grind of black pepper. Bring to a gentle boil and simmer on a very low heat until the sauce has thickened – approximately 7-10 minutes.

5.   If using whole almonds rather than flaked almonds, you'll need to 'blanch' them (remove the skins). To do this, place the almonds in a bowl, pour over boiling water until covered. After 1-minute, drain the almonds, rinse with cold water, then place on a kitchen towel. Once dry, the skins should be easy to slip off using your fingers. To toast them, simply melt a knob of butter in a frying pan, add the almonds, stir to coat and cook on a medium-heat for approximately 5 minutes, stirring occasionally so they don't burn.

6.   When ready to serve, layer the bread pieces at a bottom of a large platter or shallow dish, spoon over the yoghurt sauce, followed by the tomato sauce, then arrange the aubergine chunks on top and garnish with parsley, thin slices of red chilli, pomegranate seeds (if using) and the toasted almonds. Finish with a drizzle of olive oil.

This dish is a real crowd-pleaser, and stress-free if you're the chef in charge. Sami says that all the components of fattet can be made in advance (even a day before), so at crunch time the only thing left to do is assemble.

FATTET MAKDOUS

ILLUSTRATION BY TAMARA QUSHHA تمارا قُشحة

Some wave sticks from below, beating and shaking branches until the olives fall to the earth.

ARRIVE IN PALESTINE BETWEEN SEPTEMBER AND OCTOBER, AND IT'S ONLY A MATTER OF TIME UNTIL A PASSERBY IN THE STREET WILL STOP YOU AND ASK IF YOU WOULD LIKE TO JOIN THEM AND THEIR FAMILY IN PICKING OLIVES.

AS SOON AS THE DUSTY HILLS ARE CLEANSED WITH THE FIRST SHEETS OF RAIN, THEY COME ALIVE WITH COMMUNAL ACTIVITY.

JOURNALIST AND REGULAR SKATEPAL VOLUNTEER, TESSA FOX, PROVIDES A LITTLE MORE CONTEXT BEHIND THE HUMBLE OLIVE.

[LEFT] **The grippy vulcanised sole of skate shoes turns out to be pretty good for scaling olive trees too. Nablus area, 2019.** PHOTO BY TOM BIRD.

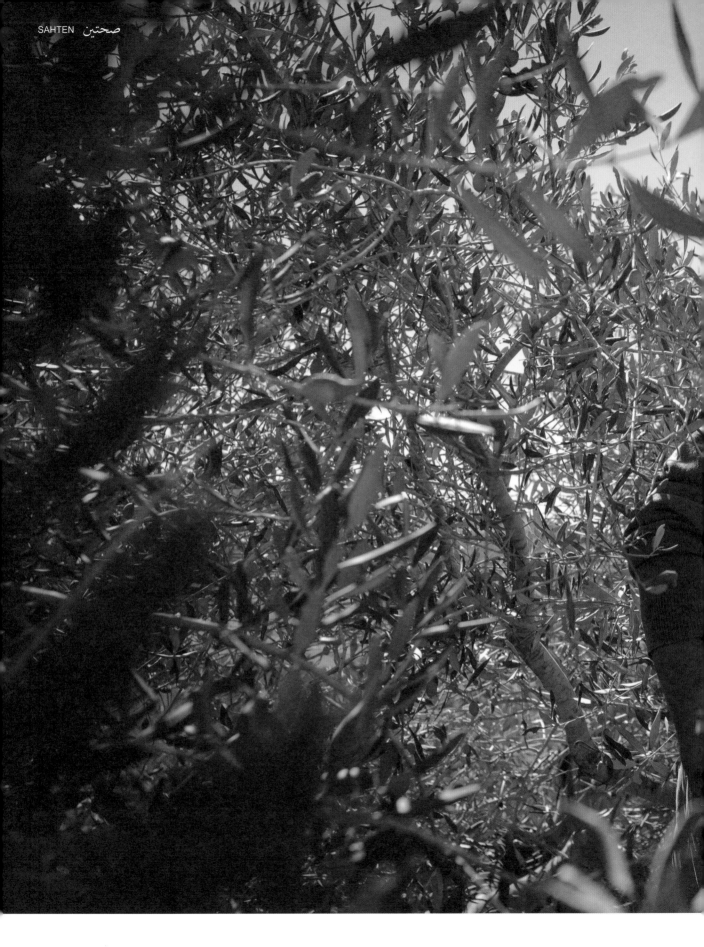

Kindness, generosity and patience is what enabled Asira's concrete skatepark to finally be built in 2015. Especially from local Sammy Samir, who hosted much of the international team at his house during construction. We've been repaying the favour during harvest season ever since. 2015. PHOTO BY EMIL AGERSKOV.

After a long dry summer, the first rainfall in October brings with it a refreshing coolness and washes away the thick settled dust from the trees of Palestine.

The change of season also marks the commencement of the olive harvest, a time of community, family togetherness and a celebration of Palestinian culture.

The olive tree appears as a recurring pattern across the rocky hills of central Palestine. Curving around the slopes, the olive groves are planted in cascading terraces, some of which were built thousands of years ago. Al Walaja, a village near Bethlehem, is in fact home to what is said to be the oldest olive tree in the world. Named 'Al Badawi', the ancient tree has been growing for somewhere between 4,000 and 5,000 years, and measures 12 meters in radius and 11 meters high.

During the olive harvest, the trees are in movement as the most able of the family climb onto branches or perch on ladders to rake or hand pick the oil-rich fruit. Some wave sticks from below, beating and shaking branches until the olives fall to the earth. Tarpaulin sheets are laid in the shade of the tree, ready to collect the fallen fruit, which are then piled into buckets and loaded into cars or trucks, destined to be pressed. Some of the younger generation lament this labour-intensive time of year as their family calls for assistance in their

The grandmother of local skaters Lara, Sireen and Noha demonstrates the correct way to remove excess leaves from the days harvest. PHOTO BY JON BARKER.

SkatePal volunteers are invited to sit down and break bread with the family and replenish the energy stores before another few hours spent wrestling stubbon olives from the tree. Nablus area, 2019. PHOTO BY TOM BIRD.

[CONTINUED]

fields, though it is a tradition hard to reject. The olive and its tree can be said to be at the core of Palestinian identity and is repeatedly referred to in the holy books of all monotheistic religions.

The olive branch itself is an internationally recognised symbol of peace, but for Palestinians, its meaning extends into the thick trunks and roots, symbolizing the people's steadfastness and connection to the land. Furthermore, the olive tree is drought resistant and can continue to produce fruit for hundreds of years, which Palestinians see as a symbol of their resilience in spite of living under occupation.

The separation barrier – often simply referred to as 'the wall' – which commenced construction in 2002 (and continues to be illegal under international law) has since become a globally recognised icon of the bitter and worsening conflict between Israel & Palestine. One of the many consequences is that it

cuts off Palestinian farmers from their agricultural plots, often olive groves that have been tended by families for generations; a story explored in the Emmy Award-winning film '5 Broken Cameras' (2011).

Olive groves make up nearly 50% of the agricultural land in Palestine and around 14% of the total economy. For the majority of families, the olive harvest is for their own consumption. Some sell to local markets and a smaller number sell their raw product to larger, more commercial presses for export. There is generally a single olive press for each village, in which men work throughout the night among loud, mechanical sounds and the strong smell of fresh olive oil pulsing from the press into gallon drums. And if not oil and olives, then soap is another product made from the pressed fruit – particularly in Nablus, north of the West Bank, where families have been engaged in its production for over 1000 years.

[ABOVE] No matter the shape or size of the vehicle, as long as it has wheels, then during September and October, it transports olives.

[LEFT] Closed for the majority of the year, once the Yassin family open their doors and the aging olive press whirrs into life, they do not close until every last olive from the surrounding villages has been pressed.
PHOTOS BY TOM BIRD.

THE OLIVE HARVEST

THE OLIVE HARVEST

As the number of olive sacks rise, so does the mood of the pressing plant. The economic incentive cannot be ignored, though it does not compare to the unique ability of the harvest in bringing the local community together. PHOTOS BY TOM BIRD.

THE OLIVE HARVEST

Due to it's high altitude, the olives grown in areas surrounding Nablus City produce some of the highest yields in the country. These golden drums – ready to be exported around the world – begin to stack up within a week of the first rain. Asira Al-Shamaliya, 2017.
PHOTO BY SAM HUTCHINSON.

[CONTINUED]

The olive oil produced in Palestine has long been central to local cuisine. Breakfast dishes such as ful medames [PAGE 46], hummus [PAGE 54], moutabal (an aubergine dip) and labeneh (strained yoghurt-cheese) are all served with ladles of fresh olive oil on top.

Manakeesh, a fresh baked dough topped with thyme, cheese, meat or sometimes filled with spinach or potato, is also rich in olive oil. Similarly, the pizza-like dish of Musakhan, which translates to 'heated-up,' was created by Palestinian villagers to determine whose olive oil was the best.

Olive oil is also consumed through the simple and satisfying act of dipping bread in oil and then za'atar (a mixture of thyme and other spices). Small, conjoined ceramic dishes are made specifically for these partner ingredients. Naturally, olives themselves are also extensively eaten alongside other dishes, most commonly during breakfast, after being preserved in bottles for a couple of months.

As the ancient Al Badawi tree continues to bear the fruit of 5000 years of history, the olive tree stands as testimony to Palestinians' continual connection to land, ancestral stories, rich cuisine and community resistance to a changing and abrasive land.

[ABOVE] **An olive tree featured on the first SkatePal t-shirt, designed by Jon Horner.**

[RIGHT] **Local volunteer, Kareem, takes some shade under the olive branches. 2019.** PHOTO BY TOM BIRD.

THE OLIVE HARVEST

"Don't go much closer", calls Suha, as Yasmeen's hijab disappears behind a row of flowers. We're picking fresh mint in a community garden just outside of Tulkarem – home to Suha and her daughter Yasmeen. But cutting through this tranquil evening – through the dipping sun, the scent of freshly picked mint, thyme, and the distant sound of Levantine song on a car stereo – is an 8-metre high impenetrable grey block of concrete, topped with a military lookout post and garnished with razed wire.

As the sun hurries behind the separation barrier – more commonly referred to as 'the wall' – there's an unnerving sense of vulnerability. Standing at such close proximity, especially at dusk, is not a safe environment. Tonight, the herbs are simply not worth the risk.

The wall is an unmistakable scar in the landscape and lives of those who live beside it, but as its towering structure casts us all into shadow Suha begins to explain the story behind tonight's dinner...

Widely regarded as the national dish of Palestine, 'mussahkan' is said to originate from Tulkarem, and it started as little more than a way to test the quality of olive oil. The purity of the oil would reveal itself when caramelising the onions. Good quality oil maintains the same colour when heated, whereas lesser quality oils will turn a browner shade.

It's not surprising then, that this dish most commonly lands on the Palestinian table in the fall, following the olive harvest, when the oil is at its peak. Yet spiced chicken, caramelised onions and sumac generously arranged over a bed of oil-soaked-and-toasted flatbreads would sit well any time of year.

Mussakhan

– by YASMEEN & SUHA FOQHA (TULKAREM)

سهى و سها

MUSSAKHAN

Yasmeen (left) and her mother Suha (right), on their co-operative agricultural farm.
Tulkarem, 2019. PHOTO BY TOM BIRD.

Yasmeen ياسمين and her mother Suha سها are a power duo in Palestine's youth communities.

Yasmeen is an 18-year old regular shredder at Jayyous skatepark, for which her mother is the local coordinator – working with schools to develop recreational programmes and summer schools. When not at the skatepark, Yasmeen is out mobilising Palestine's – particularly female – youth groups to explore their own country, mainly by organising day-trips that involve skateboarding, hiking and even horse-riding. Check out @POWER_YOUTH_ on Instagram to see the great work Yasmeen is doing.

- **4 TABOON BREADS** (OR SIMILAR ARABIC FLATBREAD)
- **1kg CHICKEN THIGHS**
- **1kg WHITE ONION** (SLICED)
- **1L OLIVE OIL**
- **2 TBSP SUMAC**
- **2 TBSP ALMONDS** (ROUGHLY CHOPPED)
- **1 HANDFUL PARSLEY** (ROUGHLY CHOPPED)
- **SALT & PEPPER**

SERVES: **4**
PREP TIME: **1 HR**

1. Using a sharp knife, score the chicken pieces, place in a pot, salt well, then pour over cold water until just about covered. Put a lid on top and turn the hob to medium/high heat.

2. While the chicken is being brought to a boil, thinly slice the onions and pour a good glug of good quality olive oil into another pot. Throw the onions into the pot over a low/medium heat, add a few good pinches of salt and half the sumac, and cook down until they're soft and stringy. Keep topping up the oil to prevent the onions from burning.

3. Once the chicken is boiling, reduce heat to a simmer. After about 15 mins, remove the chicken from the pot, combine with the cooked onions and transfer to a baking tray. Lather with more lashings of olive oil and roast at 180°C.

4. In the meantime, fill a shallow bowl with olive oil and dunk the edges of the breads. With your hands, rub some more oil over the centre of the breads. Once the chicken skin begins to crisp up, move the pieces to the bottom shelf of the oven and put the oil-dipped breads on the top shelf to crisp also.

5. Once the chicken is cooked through and the skin crispy, the onions dark purple and stringy, and the taboon breads toasted to a light brown colour, it's time to assemble. Scoop the chicken & onion mixture onto the breads – allow one per person – and finish each with another sprinkle of sumac, finely chopped parsley, a squeeze of lemon, a couple tbsps of lightly crushed almonds and, of course, one final dash of olive oil.

MUSSAKHAN

Mansaf

– by DIANA MUSA & THE MOTHER OF THE HAMADNEH FAMILY

ديانا موسى والأم من عائلة الحمادنه

(SAN FRANCISCO / ASIRA AL-SHAMALIYA)

Succulent pieces of lamb, scattered over turmeric-spiced rice, garnished with toasted almonds, drenched in 'jameed', to be scooped up with paper-thin markook bread. 'Mansaf' is said to have originated from the nomadic Bedouin tribes of the Levant, and has since become the national dish of Jordan. It is not uncommon however, to find it being prepared across Palestine – and given that Jordan hosts the world's largest number of Palestinian refugees, its cultural fluidity is hardly surprising.

Sourcing the recipe for these pages, however, required patience and endeavour. Originally suggested by SkatePal volunteer Diana Musa, the recipe took its first twists and turns following the advice of four elderly ladies in Nablus. It was later amended again by Sawsan Yaseen, a neighbour to the volunteer apartment in Asira (and lender of cooking pots), before being completely re-worked by Em Mohammed – the mother of the all-skater Hamadneh family – who promptly kicked Diana out from the SkatePal kitchen to make it 'the authentic way'.

In this case, Diana has consolidated generations of advice into one single recipe, cutting preparation time to approximately 1hr, rather than the four additional hours of conversation about family, top-ups of coffee, demonstrations with imaginary kitchen utensils, and photos of prospective husbands.

Diana Musa ديانا موسى is an American skater of Palestinan heritage, whose family sought asylum during the 1948 'Nakba', after being displaced from their original home in Lifta; which stands now as an abandoned village on the outskirts of Jerusalem. She currently lives in San Francisco, where she works for Lowcard Skate Magazine and organises womens skate sessions for the local community.

– 300g **LONG GRAIN RICE**
– 1kg **THICK CUT LAMB PIECES**
 (WITH BONES IF POSSIBLE)
– 1L **NATURAL YOGHURT**
 (MADE FROM SHEEP OR GOAT
 MILK IF POSSIBLE)
– 1 **WHITE ONION** (DICED)
– 2 **BAY LEAVES**
– 1 **HANDFUL OF PINE NUTS**
– 1 **HANDFUL OF ALMONDS**
– 1 **TBSP TURMERIC**
– 1 **TBSP CARDAMOM PODS**
 (OPTIONAL)
– **SALT & PEPPER**
– 1 **HANDFUL OF PARSLEY**
 (ROUGHLY CHOPPED)
– 2-3 **SPRIGS OF MINT**
 (ROUGHLY CHOPPED)
– **BAG OF 'MARKOOK' BREAD**
 (OR SIMILAR VERY THIN BREAD)

SERVES: **8**
PREP TIME: **1 HR**

1. Wash the rice in a colander. Then leave to soak in cold water for around 20 minutes before draining.

2. In a large pot, add a glug of oil and sweat the onion on a low heat. Rinse the lamb under cold water and remove any excess fat, then place the meat in the pot with the onion and bay leaves, and top with water until just covered. Bring to a boil.

3. Reduce the heat to a simmer and cover with a lid, allowing steam to escape. Cook for around 30 minutes, checking every so often to skim any fat from the top of the water.

4. Warm a splash of olive oil in a frying pan and lightly fry both the pine nuts and almonds until browned. Set to one side, then in the same oil, add ½ the turmeric and the drained rice and flash-fry for a couple of minutes, until the rice is coated a nice yellow colour.

5. Once the meat is cooked, DON'T drain the broth from the pot... this is crucial to the flavours of mansaf. Instead, pour ½ of the broth into a seperate pot, add the rice and simmer until cooked.

6. Meanwhile, add the yoghurt, mint and remaining turmeric to the pot with the lamb. Season with salt & pepper and turn to a low heat, stirring until everything is coated.

Rather than yoghurt, authentic mansaf is made with 'jameed' – a traditional Bedouin product made from goats milk which is heavily salted, wrung out in muslin cloth and sun-dried for a few days, creating a tough, easily preserved ball of cheese. This is near impossible to find outside of the Levant, however a tub of plain yoghurt mixed with 1tsp of salt will suffice as a substitute.

7. Now to combine it all... grab a large serving plate (an old wide deck stripped of its griptape is a handy alternative) and create a layer of shredded markook bread as the base. Top with the rice (and if you have any spare broth, pour it over). Next, add pieces of lamb along with some spoonfuls of the yoghurt sauce (pour any excess sauce into a separate bowl). Finish by scattering the toasted pine nuts, almonds, cardamom pods and chopped parsley over the top, then attack it like Grant Taylor would some pool coping.

Diana Musa, Asira Al-Shamaliya, 2019. PHOTO BY TOM BIRD.

MANSAF

[LEFT] Sireen and Ledia practicing rock-fakies together at Asira skatepark.

[RIGHT] SkatePal volunteers Lauren Bouza and Kim Butter take a nap at a former
water park turned skatespot near the **Dead Sea.** PHOTOS BY BEN BRAVENEC.

Harry Stonebridge, drop in, Ramallah plaza. Legend has it that he spent the duration of his stay contemplating it, and finally plucked the courage the night before departing. PHOTO BY BEN BRAVENEC.

Skateboarding is fun. If you don't believe us, just ask Mohammed & Ahed Hamadneh. Asira Al-Shamaliya, 2017. PHOTO BY TOM BIRD.

Maqlubah

There are few Palestinian dishes that can match the theatre of the maqlubah. The title of the dish itself is actually the Arabic translation of 'upside-down', referring to the final stage of preparation, where huge pots are dramatically flipped over upon serving.

During the annual olive harvest, you're as likely to see pots flipping up into the air, as you are to see olives falling down from it. Picking olives is tiring work after all, so the protein in the chicken helps to repair flagging arms, and the carbohydrate in the rice refuels the legs for another few hours of tree climbing.

This dish is intended for large groups, so it's no surprise that it's hugely popular on Fridays – when all the family are together at home. "All my friends eat maqlubah on Friday", says Malak, one of the keenest skateboarders in Ramallah. Due to school exams, it took a long time to get our hands on the Battatt family recipe, but if Malak's slappy 50-50s are the benchmark, then this recipe won't disappoint.

– by MALAK BATTATT ملاك بطاط
& HER MOTHER (RAMALLAH)

MAQLUBAH

ملاك بشت is a 16 year-old skater from Ramallah. Since p
first time in 2018, Malak has been a regular face at SkatePa
areyyet Youth Club, quickly becoming one of our Local V
the first to suggest skating down the city's many hills ra
f you hear the familiar sound of polyurethane on Ramallal
ind Malak close by.

Malak Battatt, local skater and volunteer at SkatePal's weekly sessions at Ramallah Youth Centre. PHOTO BY KEISHA FINAI.

- **1kg CHICKEN** (WINGS & THIGHS)
- **250g LONG-GRAIN RICE**
- **150g VERMICELLI NOODLES**
- **1 CAULIFLOWER** (CUT IN FLORETS)
- **1 AUBERGINE** (DICED)
- **2 CARROTS** (DICED)
- **2 POTATOES** (PEELED & DICED)
- **1 ONION** (CUT INTO WEDGES)
- **4 LARGE TOMATOES** (DICED)
- **1 CUCUMBER** (DICED)
- **1 LEMON**
- **1 TSP CUMIN** (GROUND)
- **1 TSP TURMERIC** (GROUND)
- **1 TSP CINNAMON** (GROUND)
- **1 TSP ALLSPICE** (GROUND)
- **1 BUNCH PARSLEY** (ROUGHLY CHOPPED)
- **1L NATURAL YOGHURT**
- **SALT & PEPPER**

SERVES: **5**
PREP TIME: **1.5 HR**

There's no secret behind flipping a giant pot of hot food upside down, every family finds their own technique, so the same applies to you. A tip though – it can require more than 1 person!

1. Start by preparing all the vegetables. Throw them all in a bowl (except the onion), season with a pinch of salt and pepper and let sit for a moment.

2. Place the rice and vermicelli noodles in a bowl, pour over a couple of cups of water and leave to soak for 20 mins before draining.

3. Place all pieces of chicken into a large pot, then add the onions wedges, cumin, bay leaves and a few big pinches of salt and pepper. Pour in enough cold water until the chicken is just covered and set over a high heat. Once the pot begins to boil reduce to a simmer.

4. In a saucepan with a good glug of good quality olive oil, begin frying the vegetables in batches until lightly browned.

5. Once all vegetables are browned and removed, add another splash of olive oil to the pan then chuck in the drained rice and noodles over a medium heat. Give them a stir and be wary of burning them (you're just cooking out the moisture) then add in the remainder of the spices. Stir well until coated and smelling fragrant.

6. Now it's time to add everything to the pot. First, drain the stock from the chicken pot into a separate jug or container. Then, leaving the cooked chicken as the base layer in the pot, add all the browned vegetables on top to make a second layer, then make a final layer with the spiced rice and noodles. Using the back of a spoon, press down and ensure the pot is compact with no gaps, then pour the stock over until it reaches roughly the same level as the rice. Cover the pot with a lid and return to the stove on a medium heat. Cook for approx 30 mins, checking every 10 minutes to give the rice layer a little stir and see if the pot needs topping up with stock. Then comes the moment all this faff has been leading up to...

7. Remove the pot from the heat and leave to stand for a few minutes before placing a large dish / tray / whatever flat object you can find over the pot. Then, in one smooth motion, flip both the pot and the dish upside down, whilst simultaneously shouting 'MACK-LOO-BAA'.

8. Tap the bottom of the pot to loosen any food stuck to it, then carefully lift the pot to reveal a steaming mountain of food. Garnish with a squeeze of lemon and some chopped parsley. Serve with a dollop of yogurt on each portion and some freshly chopped tomatoes and cucumber.

[LEFT] **Maqlubah at the family home of Hani Awwad, who for a couple of years became the de-facto Arabic teacher for many SkatePal volunteers. Awarta, 2017.** PHOTO BY TOM BIRD.

[ABOVE] **Maqlubah with the family of Basma and Jawwad, two of Asira's early rippers. If this traditional Friday feast can be prepared in a field, it shouldn't be too daunting in your kitchen. Asira Al-Shamaliya, 2019.** PHOTO BY OWEN GODBERT.

Malak helps new starter, Nadeen, with her balance rolling in and out of basic grinds at Ramallah Youth Centre, 2019. PHOTO BY KEISHA FINAI.

Oh, kanafeh… big golden wheel of sweet cheesy joy. This dessert – made of melted goat's cheese, crowned with toasted semolina crust and doused in rose-water sugar syrup – is eaten all over the Arab world. But unlike many Arab dishes, whose origins are repeatedly discussed and disputed, few will disagree that this delicacy hails from Nablus – a city at the heart of the Palestinian West Bank, and a short ride over the hill from SkatePal's long-standing Asira skatepark.

Under the shadow of the Al Kebir mosque, deep in the souk of the Old City, you'll find no grand entrance, or any indication about what this otherwise ordinary doorway opens to, that is, until a fresh golden disc is hastily transported from the door across the street. And at once, like an apparition, crowds appear, feast, and disperse. Al-Aqsa kanafeh has become a rite of passage for anyone within the SkatePal team.

Abu Hamdi, the astute face of Al-Aqsa, leads a busy life dedicated to keeping the hungry crowds at bay with his trusty kanafeh slicer. Luckily, this recipe comes courtesy of Tayseer, an Asira local who has been around long enough to know a thing or two about the Palestinian delicacy.

Kanafeh

– by TAYSEER HAMADNEH (ASIRA AL-SHAMALIYA)

تايسير حمادنه

[LEFT] Wheels of pre-prepared knafeh await the stove. There are variations on the recipe, for example these are topped with a type of shredded wheat, however the classic version (featured in this book) is made with semolina. PHOTO BY TOM BIRD.

[RIGHT] Abu-Hamdi, Al Aqsa. It's safe to assume this man might hold the world record for having made more knafeh that any other human. A fresh batch lasts a minute at most, before another wheel is promply delivered to the delight of baying crowd. Nablus Old City, 2019. PHOTO BY JAMES MCGARRAGLE.

Tayseer M Hamadneh. Half man, half moustache.
PHOTO BY TOM BIRD.

"God gave me everything, so I want to give it back", says Tayseer تايسير, as he lightly presses semolina into the edges of the pan. He is characterised as much by his trademark handlebar moustache and farmer's cap, as he is by the warm aura that surrounds him the moment he enters the room. As a descendant of the first family to construct a house in Asira 380 years ago, Tayseer commands a degree of respect from his fellow countrymen. Not only is he an advocate of kanafeh – regularly showing volunteers how to make it – he's been a big advocate of SkatePal's work since day one. Although he doesn't skate himself, Tayseer sees the benefits that skateboarding can bring to young people in the village and surrounding areas, often visiting the skatepark to see how the classes are going.

– 500g **SEMOLINA DURUM WHEAT** (YELLOW FLOUR)
– 500g **NABULSI CHEESE** (SUB FOR A 2:1 RATIO MIX OF FRESH MOZZARELLA & RICOTTA)
– 300ml **WATER**
– 300g **CASTER SUGAR**
– 1 PACK **GHEE / LARD / BUTTER** (ENOUGH TO GREASE THE PAN)
– 100g **UNSALTED PISTACHIOS** (OPTIONAL)

SERVES: **12**
PREP TIME: **30 MINS**

As with mansaf, kanafeh too is made using a very particular cheese (Nablusi or Akkawi) which is near impossible to source outside of the Levant. Nevertheless, combining fresh mozzarella and ricotta will give a plausible alternative.

1. To make the sugar syrup: add the water and sugar to a pan, bring to a boil, then reduce to a simmer for a couple of minutes, allowing it to thicken slightly. Remove from the heat and leave to cool.

2. Remove the pistachios from their shells and crush using a pestle & mortar if you have one, otherwise wrap in cling film or paper and use a hammer / old urethane wheel to crush.

3. Mix 2 tbsp melted ghee (or butter) and 2 tbsp sugar syrup (doesn't matter if it's still hot) into the semolina and mix with your hands until it has a similar texture to cous-cous.

4. Next, grease your baking dish / frying pan with ghee, and line it with the semolina mixture, pressing down lightly with your fingers until compacted.

5. Arrange the ricotta and mozzarella mix evenly across the top, allowing a perimeter for the cheese to melt into.

6. The cooking process requires a bit of skill... Switch the stove to a low heat. If using a big dish, place on top and continuously rotate it over the flame until you see the edges begin to turn a dark orange – the aim is to evenly cook the semolina base until it's golden, but not burnt. If using a frying pan, treat it like an omelette.

7. Once the edges are changing colour and the cheese is melting, remove from the heat. Place a similar sized dish / plate over the top of the dish / pan and flip upside down, hopefully revealing the perfect golden crust (inshallah).

8. Finish by drizzling the sugar syrup over the top, and garnish with the crushed pistachios.

"Sometimes, when I can't

[LEFT] Same moustache, same farmer's cap, same silver dish. Tayseer is a man of tradition. 2016. PHOTO BY OWEN GODBERT.

[RIGHT] Kanafeh is traditionally prepared in a large metallic dish such as this. We won't judge you if you don't use one, but Tayseer might. PHOTO BY TOM BIRD.

sleep, I make kanafeh."

Ryan and his broken pinky explore the streets of Ramallah, 2019.
PHOTO BY CLEMENT LE GALL.

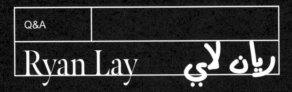

Ryan Lay is a professional skateboarder, whose numerous trips out to Palestine in recent years have naturally led him to become an ambassador for SkatePal. He's one of a growing breed of skaters to recognise that filling your body with beer and cigarettes doesn't actually bode well for a physically demanding activity where injuries are the norm. In 2019, he was nominated for Thrasher Magazine's prestigious 'Skater of the Year', so as one of skateboarding's gnarliest foodies, we thought he could share his thoughts on skating and nutrition.

SkatePal: SO... FOOD. WHAT'S YOUR RELATIONSHIP WITH IT?

Ryan Lay: Love it. I grow food in the garden, cook every day and am especially interested in the cultural and healing powers of food. This wasn't something I was always interested in but having been vegan the past decade or so I've really opened myself up to thinking about food beyond merely just energy.

HOW ARE YOUR CULINARY SKILLS? YOU WERE BLESSED WITH SKATEBOARDING, SO TECHNICALLY YOU'RE NOT ALLOWED BOTH...

I'm what you might call a pragmatic cook. I usually make a bulk legume recipe in the insta-pot (hummus, lentil dish, black beans) and some sort of grain at the beginning of the week, overnight oats for breakfast, and a lot of green or chocolate smoothies in the Vitamix. I wish I had more patience to learn how to bake and cook more involved recipes but aside from that I usually just end up sautéing a bunch of veggies.

WHAT FIRST BROUGHT YOU TO PALESTINE?

I first visited Palestine in 2018 just as a tourist. I had posted a wonderful Angela Davis book on Palestine and Ferguson on my Instagram story, and Maen Hammad (local coordinator for SkatePal) reached out to me and extended an invite. A few months later I was on a flight there after a trip to Europe and ended up skating with him, Aram and Adham (some of the first skaters in the West Bank) for a couple of weeks.

WHAT DID YOU THINK OF FOOD IN PALESTINE? WAS IT TOUGH TO MAINTAIN A VEGAN DIET?

I guess what some would refer to as Mediterranean cuisine here has long been a comfort food for me and I typically eat at a local Syrian or Lebanese restaurant on a weekly basis here in Arizona. Exceeding even my high expectations, the food totally blew me away. Usually food on skate trips can be a little tough or just rushed through, but in Palestine you really have to set aside time to enjoy everything it has to offer.

ANY STAND-OUT FOOD EXPERIENCES?

Aram's aunt made us a vegan and non-vegan pot of upside-down rice, or Maqluba, which was incredible. It was just a towering and delicious rice dish with all sorts of fried veggies.

"Usually food on skate trips can be a little tough or just rushed through, but in Palestine you really have to set aside time to enjoy everything on offer."

Ryan riding into a don't-look-down 50-50. Ramallah, 2019.
PHOTO BY CLEMENT LE GALL

If all else fails, expose your body to the healing powers of fresh corn. It might not cure broken bones, but it will at least put a smile on your face. Ramallah, 2019.
PHOTO BY CLEMENT LE GALL.

"It goes without saying, but standing at a bar drinking beers on a swollen ligament is about the worst thing you can do."

SKATERS SEEM TO BE TAKING A MORE HOLISTIC VIEW. WARM-UP STRETCHES WERE ONCE MET WITH A RAISED EYEBROW, BUT MORE SKATERS THAN EVER ARE CITING YOGA, PHYSIOTHERAPY AND CLEAN EATING AS PART OF THEIR PROGRESSION. WHY THE SHIFT?

Yeah I think in general the median age of pro skaters has gone up and as a result of that people are looking for ways to extend their careers and just general ability to skate. There's also just more space for varying approaches to skating, which has been a really great thing for the culture.

BEING ACCEPTED INTO THE OLYMPICS HAS BOLSTERED THE SPORTING CREDENTIALS OF SKATEBOARDING, SO WILL DIETARY REGIME BECOME AS IMPORTANT TO FUTURE SKATEBOARDERS AS THE BOARD THEY'RE RIDING?

I think so. As skating becomes more institutionalized and also injected with serious corporate cash, we're going to see more and more skaters modeling themselves after big time athletes to optimize their performance. That means personal trainers, nutrition counseling, regimented exercises and all that jazz.

INJURY IS PART OF THE PARCEL WHEN IT COMES TO SKATEBOARDING. AS A PROFESSIONAL SKATEBOARDER, YOU'VE TAKEN YOUR FAIR SHARE OF KNOCKS. HOW DOES DIET (OR GENERAL BODY MAINTENANCE) IMPACT RECOVERY?

It's hard to gauge. I'm no nutritionist, but certainly the placebo effect of being considerate towards your body and making the effort helps. It goes without saying, but standing at a bar drinking too many beers on a swollen ligament is about the worst thing you can do, and something I think many of us are guilty of.

IN 2019, YOU WERE NOMINATED FOR ONE OF SKATEBOARDING'S ULTIMATE ACCOLADES: THRASHER'S SKATER OF THE YEAR. PROOF THAT EATING YOUR GREENS PAYS OFF...

It was a huge surprise and honestly really great to get that kind of recognition. Hailing from Arizona, I live far from the epicenter of skating so I always kind of feel like an outsider.

AS WELL AS BEING AN AMBASSADOR FOR SKATEPAL'S PROJECTS, YOU RUN A PROGRAMME BACK IN THE U.S. CALLED SKATE AFTER SCHOOL. CAN YOU TELL US A LITTLE MORE ABOUT THIS AND WHAT IT HAS TAUGHT YOU ABOUT THE IMPACT SKATEBOARDING CAN HAVE?

Skate After School is a non-profit I started with a couple friends to provide programming for underserved youth using refurbished skate equipment. It has blossomed into a small organisation that serves roughly 250 kids a week across eight low-income elementary schools and honestly has been one of the joys of my life. Working with youth and in your local community always helps to re-stoke the fire. Skating is an immensely powerful tool that ties in creativity, athleticism and community – it's up to all of us to make sure it's accessible to anyone who wants to have a go at it.

IF YOU CAN COMPARE YOUR STYLE OF SKATING TO A MEAL – WHAT WOULD IT BE?

Haha oh boy. Let's go with a vegetarian mezze platter–light with something for everyone!

02-2770261

Shisha-to-nosegind. Now go and search 'Ryan Lay in Palestine' online to watch the edit from his skate trip around the West Bank. PHOTO BY CLEMENT LE GALL.

This series of icons have been collected from the entrances of various food vendors all across Palestine. It's not clear which was the original face of certified quality. Nor is it clear from where he originated – as the face appears to subtly morph between classic depictions of an Italian pizza chef, to Turkish doner chef, to Japanese sushi chef. What is clear however, is that any time you see this guy giving you the sign, you can rest assured that deliciousness awaits…

The illustrations accompanying each recipe throughout this book have been created in collaboration with various children from SkatePal's programmes in Palestine, as well as the Palestinian dispora in Canada.

Noor Abouseido نور ابوسيدو is a Palestinian-Canadian skater and animator, whose family fled Gaza and settled in Ottawa, Canada. During her time volunteering with SkatePal in 2019, we asked Noor to help in illustrating each dish for the book. She printed her outline sketches and handed out copies to the kids at the skatepark, allowing them to colour the drawings however they pleased. The results of which are what you see in the pages of this book.

A massive thanks to all the habibis and habibtis (listed below) that contributed their artistic talents. Look out for some of their faces throughout the rest of the book!

LARA YASEEN	لارا ياسين
NOHA YASEEN	نها ياسين
SEREEN YASEEN	سرين ياسين
LEDIA SAWWALHA	ليديا صوالحه
ASENAT SAWWALHA	أسينات صوالحه
KARAM	گرم
JEHAD ABUHASAN	جهاد ابو حسن
MOHAMMAD HAMADNEH	محمد حمادنه
MALIK HAMADNEH	مالك حمادنه
TARNEEM HAMADNEH	ترنيم حمادنه
AHED HAMADNEH	عهد حمادنه
MAJD ABOU-SEIDO	مجد ابوسيدو
MIRA ABOU-SEIDO	ميرا ابوسيدو

Thanks Shukran
شكراً

A huge thank you to everyone who has supported SkatePal over the years – all the volunteers, skaters, shops, magazines and companies who have helped us in any way big or small, we wouldn't be here without you.

An extra special thank you to repeat volunteer Tom Bird, for not only his dedication in pulling together the content of this book, but his tireless patience in piecing it together, for free, during a global pandemic.

SkatePal team, past and present:

CHARLIE DAVIS

THEO KRISH

ARAM SABBAH

DOROTHY ISKRZYNSKA

ALEX ADETIBA

ANNA FARELLO

NELSON BEESLEY

MAEN HAMMAD

PHIL JOA

CHRIS JONES

RYAN LAY

DANI ABULHAWA

SkatePal family:

MAJD RAMADAN

ABDULLAH MILHEM

OMAR HATTAB

EIHAB TAHA

OSAMA TITI

ADHAM TAMIMI

MAI ALEM

AMR KHOURY

GEORGE KAILEH

SALAMEH KAILEH

BASAM WADI

SAJED ABU-ULBA

MALAK BATTATT

KAREEM BARAKAT

To all of our recipe contributors:

AMR & MUHANED (AL AMAD & SONS)

ABU ALI SAWALMA

TESSA FOX

JOSH SUTTON

JESS HOWE & MEGAN MAULE (WHAT THE FATTOUSH)
www.whatthefattoush.com
@whatthefattoush

A special thanks to What The Fattoush for their help in shaping the recipes – providing a chef's eye over our notes to produce clear, formulated and consistent instructions.

IZZELDIN BUKHARI (SACRED CUISINE)
www.sacred-cuisine.com
@sacredcuisine

MOATH & NADA QASHOO & THE HIBA FAMILY
www.hiba-express.co.uk/mini-hiba
@hibaexpress / @minihibae17

SAMI TAMIMI
Feeling inspired? Go buy his book 'Falastin', published 2019 by Penguin Random House.

ABOOD BARHAN

ARAM & SORIDA SABBAH

YASMEEN & SUHA FOQHA

DIANA MUSA

EM HAMADNEH

MALAK BATTATT

TAYSEER M. HAMADNEH

To our interviewees:

RYAN LAY
Be sure to check out the 'Vent City' podcast, which Ryan hosts with a panel of characters who seek to cover 'the interesting stuff happening on the peripheries of skateboarding'.

WALA QAMHIEH

ARAM SABBAH
Also check out Aram in the Globally Stoked panel discussion at Pushing Boarders skateboarding conference in Malmö, Sweden (2019). All talks are available to view online.

To our photographers:

TOM BIRD

OWEN GODBERT

EMIL AGERSKOV

SAM HUTCHINSON

PAULA GRANT

WILL JIVCOFF

CLEMENT LE GALL

DIANA MUSA

LOÏC LAFORGE

KEISHA FINAI

JULIAN MAEHRLEIN

SAM ASHLEY

BEN BRAVENEC

ANIL ILTAS

JOHN BARKER

TOMAS PAJDLHAUSER

JAMES MCGARRAGLE

DOROTHY ISKRZYNSKA

JAMES HOLMAN

JOHNNY MCMULLAN

REID ALLEN

To our illustrators:

NOOR ABOU-SEIDO

MAJD ABOU-SEIDO

MIRA ABOU-SEIDO

LARA YASEEN

NOHA YASEEN

SEREEN YASEEN

LEDIA SAWWALHA

ASENAT SAWWALHA

MOHAMMAD HAMADNEH

MALIK HAMADNEH

TARNEEM HAMADNEH

AHED HAMADNEH

KARAM

JEHAD ABUHASAN

And to anyone who provided help along the way:

MAJDAL SOBAH

AHMAD IDEA

TAMARA QUSHHA

KEIKO OIKAWA

JONAH AINSLIE

JEAN KELTIE

THE YASSIN FAMILY (ASIRA)
Abu Tahir, Tahir & Samir for allowing us into, and showing us around, their olive pressing plant in Asira Al-Shamaliya.

When sourcing ingredients for the recipes in this book, here are some brands to look out for, which directly support farmers across the Palestinian Occupied Territories.

YAFFA
Yaffa sells Palestinian products such as dates, olive oil, herbs, spices and much more through their website and in various supermarkets across Europe.

www.yaffa.co.uk

ZAYTOUN
Zaytoun is a social enterprise organisation which sells fairtrade Palestinian products.

www.zaytoun.org

SkatePal uses skateboarding as a positive outlet for young people in Palestine. 100% of the profits made from this book are dedicated to achieving our mission of supporting, nurturing and eventually creating a self-sustaining skateboard scene in Palestine.

For more info, find us online:
www.skatepal.co.uk

Or get in touch:
info@skatepal.co.uk

Editorial team:
CHARLIE DAVIS
THEO KRISH
ARAM SABBAH
DOROTHY ISKRZYNSKA
TOM BIRD

Concept:
TOM BIRD

Design & Art direction:
TOM BIRD
www.tom-bird.com

Self-published by:
SKATEPAL
©2020

Printed in the United Kingdom.

Registered organisation: SC044815

UK Office: The Old Fire Station, 61 Leswin Road, London, N167NX

'SAHTEN'

ﺻﺤﺘﻴﻦ

MAY THE FOOD BRING YOU HEALTH

صحّة

TWO HEALTHS

PHOTO BY TOMAS PAJDLHAUSER, NABLUS, 2019.

PHOTO BY SAM ASHLEY, ASIRA AL-SHAMALIYA, 2019.

PHOTO BY ANIL ILTAS, ASIRA AL-SHAMALIYA, 2019.

PHOTO BY JAMES HOLMAN, RAMALLAH, 2019.

PHOTO BY TOM BIRD, THE DEAD SEA, 2017.